W9-BKQ-066

Guidance Services in the SECONDARY SCHOOL

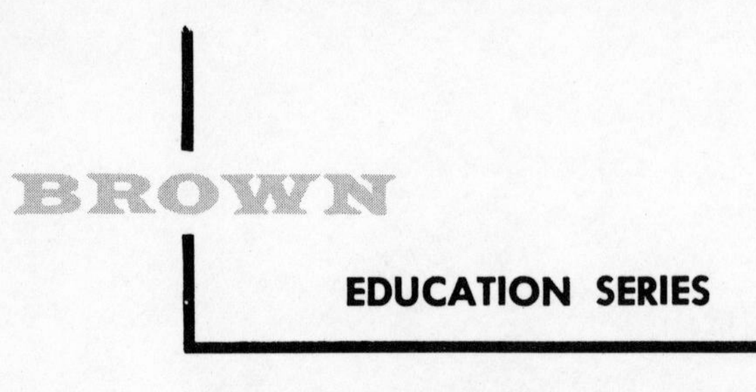

Edited by LOWRY W. HARDING, *Ph. D.,*
The Ohio State University, Columbus, Ohio

Guidance Services in the

SECONDARY SCHOOL

RAYMOND N. HATCH
Professor of Education
Michigan State University

PAUL L. DRESSEL
Professor and Director
Institutional Research
Michigan State University

JAMES W. COSTAR
Associate Professor and Chairman
Guidance and Personnel Services
Michigan State University

Library of Congress Catalog Card Number: 63-17603

Manufactured by WM. C. BROWN CO. INC., Dubuque, Iowa
Printed in U. S. A.

Preface

The major goal of American public education has always been to help each student develop his potentialities to the maximum while, at the same time, preserving the uniqueness of his own personality. Admission to our schools of students coming from a variety of backgrounds and with a wide range of interests and abilities has made this an extremely difficult task. Over the years that aspect of the school program which is directed toward helping the student make the type of adjustment which will enable him to get the most from his school experiences has gradually become known as *guidance.* Guidance exists primarily in the form of specific services for students to assist them in developing an accurate understanding of themselves and their relationship to the environment.

This book is a revision of an earlier one, *Guidance Services in the Secondary School.* It was written with two major objectives in mind. First, an attempt was made to identify the function of guidance services in the secondary school. Second, the authors tried to present a number of practical suggestions which would be helpful to teachers, administrators, and counselors in carrying out their responsibilities in the guidance program.

This is the second book in a series devoted to the application of guidance services. The first book in the series, *Guidance Services in the Elementary School,* was written primarily for school personnel responsible for guidance activities through the sixth grade. This volume has been prepared for the junior and senior high school staff. The two books have been written in parallel fashion. The format of each is essentially the same, but the contents have been modified in order to eliminate unnecessary overlap in presenting the most appropriate approach to the development and application of these services for each school level.

The book is intended as a handbook for teachers, counselors, and administrators as well as a textbook for those students who are in an introductory course in guidance. It is an extensive revision with several completely new sections. The entire content has been brought up to date and put in a form which the authors feel will make the material clear and easy to understand. Philosophical concepts have been kept at a minimum to permit more space for practical suggestions. It has been written for easy reference to specific guidance techniques and should prove quite helpful when used either as a handbook or textbook.

The authors are indebted to many individuals for their assistance and encouragement. A special note of appreciation is extended to Eleanor Ratigan for her willingness to read the manuscript and to all those teachers and counselors whose thoughtful comments and suggestions led to this revision.

January, 1963

Raymond N. Hatch
Paul L. Dressel
James W. Costar

Contents

Unit I

The Role of Guidance Services

"America, the Land of Opportunity." For over three centuries this has been the clarion cry heard around the world. The voices of the immigrant and the native born have joined in the hue attesting to the potentialities of this great land. True, there are some limitations. There have been mistakes and some individuals have been disillusioned, but the most bigoted cynic dares not deny the vast opportunities for accomplishment to be found in America.

The pioneering spirit which has pervaded the American populace has had its roots of origin in many areas. The great achievements of the individual citizen as well as the collective successes of the total population have come as a result of many influences. To single out one influence and give it credit for the amazing progress of our country is neither realistic nor possible. If one looks for the major influences, then several stand out and among them is education. Education is the means by which our people have been able to profit from the past and experiment with the future. It has helped us reduce our inner conflicts and achieve harmonious group effort. It has increased the effectiveness of our communications, resulting in greater effectiveness in all of our pursuits. Much more can be said for the value of education to our country, but most important of all, it is an opportunity in itself.

It has been the inherent privilege of American youth to be born into a society which believes that each person should have an opportunity for education, an education which will provide him with tools of understanding so that he can make the greatest individual growth possible. As the result of the development of each individual, our nation has always been near its maximum level of growth. To test the effectiveness of this belief, one needs only to look about him to see the results. No better evidence is necessary to prove the value of educational opportunity for all.

guidance services in the secondary school

The early schools of America developed under the influence of two major factors. The founding fathers had been reared in the English educational tradition and therefore thought in terms of an educational offering characterized by the schools of England. The second influence was one of expediency, as the early settlers were forced to devote their major energies to earning a living in the wilderness. This left them with little time or inclination for educational pursuits beyond the very basic fundamentals needed for communication and elementary business transactions. Nevertheless, schools were started for those who sought knowledge beyond such basic fundamentals and can be thought of as our first secondary schools.

Secondary education in America is often described as having developed in three distinct and unique increments, the Latin grammar school, the academy, and the present-day comprehensive high school. Each of these phases added to the contribution of its predecessor in attempting to meet the needs of American youth. The extent of improvement in each case can be debated at considerable length, but it must be noted that in a relatively short period of time young America did become cognizant of its changing society and made an effort to keep abreast of its educational needs.

EARLY SCHOOLS

The Latin grammar school is often considered to be our first secondary school. It was a school designed to prepare young men for such vocations as law, medicine, and the ministry. The curriculum consisted of Latin, Greek, and rhetoric, and the methods of presentation were characterized by constant drill and rigid discipline. It served a distinct purpose at that particular time, but our rapidly developing society was soon ready for a change.

The American academy appeared on the educational scene in Philadelphia and was the first American school to be entirely free from denominational or religious control. At the time Benjamin Franklin first conceived of this new educational approach, it represented a major change in the emphasis in secondary education. Such practical subjects as navigation, surveying, and business arithmetic made up the curriculum of the academies. Other innovations included admission of girls to the school and supervision by the lay public in the administration of the school program. This represented a more functional point of view than that of the Latin grammar school and was enthusiastically received by the youth of the day. As more of the new schools developed, however, the demand to retain the classical emphasis of the grammar school became very strong. Gradually the two curriculums were fused, and the functional educational offerings of the academy became more and more obscured.

Near the middle of the nineteenth century our present concept of secondary education was born in the form of the high school. The first high school was started in Boston and was dedicated to the ideal that secondary education should be free to the youth of America and should be functional. From this beginning there was soon almost universal acceptance of the high school, for it is replete with the philosophical concepts which have served from the beginning as basic elements in the governmental structure of our nation.

objectives of secondary education

Any educational practice, if it is to be accepted, must be based on an objective or set of objectives. The student of education is well aware of the wide variety of philosophies expounded by educational philosophers both past and contemporary. Each philosophy is believed by some to meet the educational needs of mankind. They differ primarily in the methods employed and what are believed to be the needs of society. Each school of thought has a following of individuals ready to debate the virtues of their particular point of view at every opportunity. It is not the intent of the authors of this text to discuss the merit of one or more of the various ideologies, but rather to draw the reader's attention to the several statements regarding the objectives of education in the United States which have influenced our educational practices during the past half century.

One of the first sets of objectives prepared by a group of educational leaders was the one announced by the Commission on the Reorganization of Secondary Education.[1] The seven objectives of secondary education as suggested by this group were: health, command of fundamental processes, worthy home membership, vocation, civic, education, worthy use of leisure, and ethical character.

Two decades after the "Cardinal Principles" made their initial impact on educational practice, another set of objectives was presented by a group of distinguished educators. This new set of objectives was offered by the Educational Policies Commission in 1938.[2] In the judgment of this body, the objectives of education can be listed under four general classifications:

1. The Objectives of Self-Realization
2. The Objectives of Human Relationships
3. The Objectives of Economic Efficiency
4. The Objectives of Civic Responsibility

One of the most recent sets of objectives was developed by the 1960 Golden Anniversary White House Conference on Children and Youth. Recommendations were made that the curriculum provide opportunities for the student to develop appreciation and understanding, at a behavioral level, of the dignity and worth of all individuals; knowledge, understanding, and appreciation of the fine and practical arts, the humanities, and the natural, physical, and social sciences; basic skills, such as reading, writing, and the use of numbers; special abilities and talents; a healthy and realistic concept of self; the best possible physical and mental health; ability to analyze critically and constructively; constructive civic attitudes and skills; interests, attitudes, and appreciations basic to the worthy use of leisure time; insights into the ethnic and religious sources of American life; and character, discipline, responsibility, and a commitment to spiritual, ethical, and moral values.[3]

---

[1]"Cardinal Principles of Secondary Education," United States Bureau of Education, Bulletin No. 35. United States Department of the Interior. Government Printing Office. 1918.

[2]*The Purposes of Education in American Democracy.* Educational Policies Commission, National Education Association and American Association of School Administrators. Washington, D. C. 1938.

[3]Reprinted from the *Conference Proceedings* prepared for the Golden Anniversary White House Conference on Children and Youth, by permission of the National Committee for Children and Youth, copyright holders.

It is significant to note the marked similarity to be found in the three sets. What is even more significant is the degree of acceptance of the objectives voiced by our leading educators. It does not seem remiss, therefore, to draw the conclusion that we have had the same general set of educational objectives for nearly fifty years. If this conclusion is drawn, one may then ask the critical question, "To what extent have we attained our objectives?"

SUCCESS OR FAILURE

Estimating the relative degree of success of any process is exceedingly difficult, but to obtain exactness in an evaluation of the educative process is a most arduous task. Judging what has been accomplished in the various objectives of education is hampered by many different factors. Some of the primary thoughts which must be taken into consideration include the following.

1. The dynamic aspects of the environment in which each generation develops makes it inadvisable to hold a specific set of standards for a prolonged period of time.
2. The increased emphasis placed on obtaining a secondary education has increased the high school population over one hundred times in the past century. The newcomers have individual needs far beyond the expectations of the nineteenth-century educator.
3. School experiences represent but a part of the total educational experiences of today's youth. Present modes of transportation and improved methods of communication have broadened educational opportunity far beyond the confines of the conventional classroom.
4. We must have an acceptable norm for success with which to make comparisons. For example, if we are to state our success in preparing youth in the area of "Economic Efficiency," we must have an acceptable level of proficiency before exact quotations of success are possible. A norm of this type has not been established, and it seems exceedingly doubtful that one can ever be established.
5. Historically, our schools have developed autonomously. The local school district has been permitted to develop a general school program along lines dictated by local conditions. Whether this is good or bad is not the question to be discussed here, but it is important to note that thousands of

independent school districts make it difficult to establish standards for measuring the success of the program in a particular school.

Because these variables exist, one might rightly ask, "Is there a way to determine our success in reaching the objectives of education?" A plausible answer may be, "Yes, if we can find significant maladjustments of youth resulting from deficiencies in educational programs." Most schools are, however, constantly striving to help each pupil make the best possible adjustment to the learning situation in order that he can attain the highest possible development of his potential. It is with this aspect of education that the guidance program is most concerned.

early antecedents of guidance services

With the building of public high schools designed to provide equal opportunity for everyone regardless of his socio-economic status, certain problems began to appear. The thinking of many proponents of the new plan was that schools should aid a pupil in acquiring learning which he might put to immediate use. This meant that the educator must provide both a program of education to include the accepted "academic" subjects of the academy and one including some type of work experience to replace the rapidly disappearing apprenticeship system. The gaps to be filled were almost staggering. The problems of obtaining buildings, equipment, and qualified teachers were extremely difficult to overcome. The most profound problem was one of reconciling the different points of view in such a way that children would not fall victim to the clash between educational philosophies. The latter problem proved to be the most difficult to overcome; in fact, traces of the same conflict are to be found in present-day faculties. At that time, as now, there were teachers who were neither qualified nor interested in assisting students in making wise vocational choices or in recognizing school work as being more than a careful study of one of the "classics." It was probably because of the vocational problems of the high school student that the first foundations of the guidance program were laid.

Between 1906 and 1908, several people were concerned with movements designed to help students with their vocational problems. Eli Weaver, a teacher in the Boys' High School in Brooklyn, organized and managed a program for placing city boys on summer jobs. William A. Wheatley, Superintendent of Schools in Fairfield and Westport, Connecticut, and Henrietta Rodman, of the New York City Schools, developed courses in occupational information. Jesse B. Davis, principal of Detroit Central High School, spent most of his time counseling boys and girls on educational and vocational problems. Davis also instituted a program devoted to vocational and moral guidance in the English composition classes of the high school in Grand Rapids, Michigan.

In Boston, Frank Parsons was appalled by the inefficient methods of selection used by industry and by the unsatisfied need of youth choosing a vocation. Because of this conviction, he formulated his plan for a vocational guidance program and presented it to Mrs. Pauline Agassiz Shaw, who agreed to give financial support. The establishment of the Vocation Bureau, as the program was called, incorporated two aspects. It was designed (1) to assist young wage earners, or prospective wage earners, and (2) to train vocational counselors.

Parsons died just a few days before the scheduled first meeting of the Vocation Bureau, and the work was continued by his friend and colleague, Ralph Albertson. Albertson also organized and prepared Parsons' posthumous book, *Choosing a Vocation.*

One of Parson's tenets was that schools and colleges should undertake vocational counseling This philosophy was evidently held by David Stone Wheeler, a progressive educator who succeeded Parsons as director of the Bureau. When Superintendent Dr. Stratton D. Brooks of the Boston Public Schools asked for assistance in the introduction of vocational counseling in the school system, the Vocation Bureau gave its wholehearted support. This was the beginning of vocational guidance in the schools.

The Boston School's Committee on Vocational Direction, under the supervision of the Vocation Bureau, was organized in 1909. The first superintendent's report indicated that the aims were "(1) thoughtful consideration of the life-career motive on the part of parents, pupils, and teachers; (2) placement; and (3) keeping in touch with those who leave school by graduation or otherwise."[4]

In 1911 Lewis P. Nash, secretary of the committee, made several recommendations. They included a course on vocations

---

[4]Brewer, John M. *History of Vocational Guidance.* New York: Harper & Brothers Publishers, 1942 p. 77.

to be required of all students and a department of vocational guidance. It was not until 1915, however, that these recommendations were carried out; and, at the same time, the school began to require certain vocational training and work experiences of counselors before they could be approved by the board of superintendents. Several other cities in the United States were experimenting with programs similar to the work being carried on in Boston. In all of the programs the workers stressed the importance of studying the individual before training and placement, but they had few, if any, tools which could be used for the purpose of selection. This condition highlighted a major weakness in the guidance field.

During the early period of development of vocational guidance, the field of applied psychology was just beginning to establish itself. Although the two movements were completely independent, it soon became apparent that the findings of the applied psychologists were to fill an important gap in the guidance movement.

A research center in applied psychology was established at the Carnegie Institute of Technology just prior to World War I. A group of psychologists, under the direction of Walter Dill Scott and Walter V. Bingham, developed methods of measuring vocationally significant mental traits. Continued development of these tests, coupled with their widespread use by high schools and colleges after the war, contributed a great deal to the guidance program.

The United States Army also applied and improved other guidance procedures. Besides the group intelligence test, they developed occupational specifications, trade tests, and rating scales. Their qualification card has been translated for school use and is similar to our present-day cumulative record folder.

The impetus given personnel work by the army during World War I was directly responsible for the organization of many groups devoted to the study of tests and measurement. One of the most important organizations formed was the Committee on Cooperative Experiments in Student Personnel, sponsored by the American Council on Education.

Another activity which had a profound effect on the guidance field was the "Mental Hygiene Movement." Given its impetus by the renowned Adolph Meyer, it served to impress upon educators the significance of the emotional development of the child. From this emphasis, course content for teachers was organized which stressed the importance of the removal of pupil frustration as a means of improved learning.

In the first two decades of our present century the guidance field grew from many roots, but primarily from the disciplines of the three movements described earlier. Educators began to recognize the importance of the individual learner, to find ways of studying him as an individual, and to express the hope that the objectives of secondary education might be more easily attained through a guidance program. In the twenty years that followed, many guidance plans were tried, definitions presented, and disappointments voiced with some of the outcomes. In this period the field of guidance withstood the rigors of metamorphosis and eventually emerged as the professional field it is today. It now is recognized by the federal government in its financial support of counselor education; by educators in nearly all of the states through the enforcement of standards for guidance workers; by several accrediting agencies of secondary schools with significant evaluation sections devoted to guidance; by hundreds of training institutions with thousands of courses in guidance, and, most important of all, by the lay public, the parents of our next generation.

the professional field of today

The professional field of guidance services as we think of it today is one which includes elements of several basic disciplines. The fields of psychology, sociology, mental hygiene, and many others, provide the basis for the techniques suggested in a program of guidance services. The services are designed to meet the needs of the individual being served – in this text, the needs of the secondary school student. A brief review of the more common needs of students may assist the reader to recall the fundamental concepts learned from other fields.

THE COMMON NEEDS[5]

Much has been written about the common needs of man, needs that seem to be apparent at birth and are present until death, varying in intensity with the passing years. The needs can be divided into two major groups, physical and emotional. They serve as the primary motivating forces of human behavior and, as such, must be recognized and understood if the guidance worker is to be effective in improving the academic adjustment of pupils.

[5]Much of the remainder of this Unit has been adapted from Raymond N. Hatch and James W. Costar. *Guidance Services in the Elementary School.* Dubuque, Iowa: Wm. C. Brown Company Publishers, 1961.

Physical. All pupils need adequate living conditions and certain activities if their physical development is to be normal. While it seems obvious that youngsters need food, clothing, and shelter, it should be remembered that the quality of these factors and the conditions under which they are obtained may affect their value. In addition, the physical structure of the child requires certain activity if the normal processes are to reach maximum effectiveness. The deprivation of the normal physical needs often results in strong behavior reactions. It may result in damage which can never be repaired. Attention to the physical needs of students is basic to the creation of a desirable environment in which maximum mental growth can take place.

Emotional. The emotional needs of students, like their physical needs, are common to all individuals. They vary only in degree of intensity. The most common emotional needs of the human being can be divided into the following four groups:

Affection—he must feel that someone cares for him and that he is wanted.

Recognition—he must develop self-esteem through recognition by others.

Belonging—he must feel effective and valued in the social group.

Security—he must feel safe if he is to venture forward to maximum development.

When emotional needs are not completely satisfied, the pupil may exhibit many unusual behavior symptoms. Some of the most common are:

Extreme aggressiveness—he speaks and acts in a hostile manner which makes him stand out, and thus he obtains satisfaction of his need for recognition.

Illness—stuttering, allergies, headaches, and hypertension are some of the physical manifestations which may indicate that certain emotional needs have not been met.

Meekness, shyness—he is afraid to venture, or he may feel greater security in nonparticipation, and thus he draws into a shell and becomes the "model" youngster.

The effectiveness of an individual's total efforts is directly related to his ability to find an acceptable method for meeting his physical and emotional needs. The school staff which is interested in providing the best educational climate for every youngster must be constantly cognizant of the basic needs of all children.

INDIVIDUAL DIFFERENCES OF STUDENTS

An appreciation of the common needs of students is fundamental to understanding the student, but it sometimes leads to dangerous conclusions. A study of the needs of individuals has a tendency to cause the guidance worker to view the individual child in terms of what is average for this group. Although all children follow certain cycles of development, which may be slow or accelerated for a given individual, they differ one from the other in many ways. Such factors as external appearance, intelligence, and special aptitudes are but a few of the things which distinguish one child from another.

Individual differences in ability have always existed. Ancient history points out the individuals who possessed certain unusual characteristics of leadership. History also relates that, in times of scarcity, the weak were sent out to wander so that the strong might be fed. It was not until the nineteenth century that society developed a sympathetic attitude toward the less fortunate. Since then educators, psychologists, and sociologists have, through careful research, influenced society's changing attitudes about the abilities of individuals. Today we view individual differences in a much broader perspective. Individual differences are better understood and accepted. Our intent now is to discover the many ways that individuals differ, keeping in mind that each particular pattern of abilities can make a significant contribution to society. Ideally, such a contribution will prove beneficial both to him and to his society.

One individual differs from other individuals in numerous ways. Some of these differences include factors which are relatively easy to measure, while others have not yet been described in an objective manner. For example, the area of academic achievement is much easier to measure than is the area of personality. In spite of the inherent problems of gaining objectivity in measurement, it seems desirable to identify some of the most common areas of individual differences.

Achievement—scholastic performance
Anatomical—height, weight, complexion

Emotional—stability, self-reliance, poise, tact, persistence

Interests—hobbies, friends, activities

Physiological—hearing, vision acuity, endurance

Psychological—speed of reaction, speed of association, coordination

Social perspective—racial, political, religious and economic attitudes

Granted that many differences exist among individuals, the guidance worker may then ask, "To what degree do they differ?" It is easier to point out differences between individuals if the trait being analyzed lends itself to objective measurement. Since, as mentioned earlier, many of these areas are difficult to evaluate, the range of differences will remain relative. Husband[6] has reported data by Wechsler which shows the distribution of capacities. It is reproduced here in Table I. The ranges of the various factors are reported in ratio form. It can be noted that some individuals are as much as six times more effective in performing certain tasks than others. Making the school experience of each individual most meaningful implies that measures must be taken by the school to collect and analyze data about each pupil which will assist teachers in understanding how he is unique. Once the differences have been ascertained, experiences can be planned within each child's pattern of abilities which will permit him to satisfy his basic needs.

INSURING GUIDANCE SERVICES FOR ALL

Teacher-training institutions have for several decades devoted considerable course time to the teaching of factors related to the understanding of individuals. School administrators have provided in-service training programs to help teachers become more competent in working with individual students. A considerable amount of writing and reports of research related to this area can be found in the professional journals. Yet in thousands of our schools today we find no organized program for the improved academic adjustment of each pupil. There are few programs which provide the machinery for a comprehensive understanding of every individual during his entire educational experience. The responsibility for this

---

[6]Husband, Richard W. *General Psychology.* New York: Rinehart and Company, Inc., 1940, p. 301.

TABLE I

Distribution of Ranges of Capacities

Capacity	Range
Body temperature	1.03 to 1
Stature at birth	1.23 to 1
Adult stature	1.27 to 1
Duration of pregnancy	1.37 to 1
Sugar in blood	1.40 to 1
Oxygen consumption	1.53 to 1
Weight of brain	1.60 to 1
Running 60 meters	1.67 to 1
Respiratory rate	1.88 to 1
Pulse rate of adults	2.03 to 1
Blood pressure	2.03 to 1
Broad jump	2.07 to 1
Speed of inserting bolts	2.09 to 1
Simple reaction time	2.24 to 1
Simple learning	2.42 to 1
Card sorting time	2.50 to 1
Intelligence quotients	2.86 to 1
Hard learning	3.87 to 1
Polishing spoons	5.10 to 1
Time to learn a maze	6.82 to 1
Intelligence scores of high school seniors	10.55 to 1

aspect of the educational program usually rests with each teacher. Although the integrity and responsibility of the teacher in performing his or her duty is not questioned, the very nature of this additional assignment is often illogical and highly hazardous.

There are several reasons why the responsibility for helping the individual to improve his school adjustment should not be left to the discretion of individual teachers. (1) The fact that such an organization provides for understanding the individual on only an incidental basis is reason enough to question the validity of such a plan. The recognition of individual differences in pupils is left entirely to the decision of one person, the teacher. There is no system in such an organization which will guarantee each student opportunity to be understood as an individual. (2) Information about an individual should be cumulative. If each teacher creates a guidance program of his own, there is seldom a provision for continuous recording of the development and growth of the individual through his entire school experience. (3) Assigning the responsibility for student adjustment to each teacher does not permit coordination of the best efforts of all teachers. The individual differences in teachers may be as broad as those among the pupils. It is quite logical that some would make a greater contribution to a certain aspect of the guidance program than others. By utilizing the staff in the area of their greatest interest and ability, it is possible to strengthen the entire program. (4) When each teacher conducts a personal guidance program there is too much duplication of effort. The teacher's workday is a full day, and his efforts in guidance usually can be made more efficient and effective by coordinating them with those of his colleagues.

To overcome the disadvantages of an "incidental" guidance program, a coordinated program of guidance services should be established. Such a program will make it possible for the school to use the abilities and interests of all staff members to the maximum. It will make it possible for the staff members to be more effective and, at the same time, increase their enjoyment of teaching. Most important, it will establish the framework for meeting the needs and concerns of every student. The latter is the primary function of guidance services in the secondary school.

some basic concepts

The term *guidance* has been used to describe many different processes, techniques, and activities. Since it has been construed so loosely, it has given rise to many interpretations and accusations. It seems advisable to identify those concepts which undergird the contents of this text so that the reader and authors will be discussing the various tools and techniques in the same frame of reference.

A GUIDANCE PROGRAM IS A PROGRAM OF SERVICES

Many definitions of guidance can be found in the guidance literature. Most of them refer to guidance as a process or an activity which is concerned with the improved adjustment of the pupil. This would seem to be the goal of all educational experiences. The difference becomes one of relative emphasis with the exact activities of the guidance program difficult to delimit or define.

It seems more desirable to think of the guidance program as a program of *services* – services which can be defined, recognized, administered, and evaluated. It is then possible to define a guidance program as a program of services specifically designed to improve the adjustment of the individual pupils for whom it was organized. Thus, activities which have other objectives as their primary purposes would not be thought of as a part of the guidance program, even though they indirectly influenced the adjustment of the individual. An identification of the guidance services is to be found later in this unit.

GUIDANCE SERVICES ARE FOR ALL CONCERNED

A program of guidance services is intended for every pupil of the school. The program is of direct help to the staff, community, and other agencies as well.

GUIDANCE SERVICES ARE FOR ALL SCHOOL LEVELS

If a guidance program is to be most effective, it must serve the pupil when he enters the school for the first time and be of assistance to him during his entire school experience.

GUIDANCE SERVICES ARE PRIMARILY PREVENTATIVE IN NATURE

Prevention of problems is a primary goal of the guidance program. Discovering minor obstacles and helping the youngster overcome them before they create major problems is the objective of an effective guidance program. This does not mean that the guidance worker avoids problems of maladjustment, but rather that they are placed in a secondary position using the rationale that "an ounce of prevention is worth a pound of cure."

THE TEACHER PLAYS A MAJOR ROLE IN THE GUIDANCE PROGRAM

The teacher in the secondary school plays a vital role in the successful operation of a program of guidance services. The teacher is in a strategic position to collect valuable information about each student and at the same time is in control of the major portion of a student's school environment. The latter situation lends itself to meaningful group guidance activities and makes it possible to help meet the basic needs of an individual through curricular experiences.

THE PROGRAM OF GUIDANCE SERVICES NEEDS TRAINED PERSONNEL

In spite of the interest and qualifications of the classroom teacher to offer the very best school experiences for every pupil, it often becomes apparent that trained assistance is needed. Such help should come from an individual or individuals trained to offer needed remedial or therapeutic aid which is beyond the training, qualifications, or the time of the classroom teacher.

THE PROGRAM OF GUIDANCE SERVICES REQUIRES COORDINATION

If all pupils are to have a similar opportunity to profit from the guidance services, and if such services are to be administered in an effective manner, coordination of the guidance activities of all persons within a school is necessary. In addition, the guidance program in one secondary school should be a part of the total school program which includes all elementary schools, junior and senior high schools, and the junior college as well.

THE GUIDANCE PROGRAM USES AND IMPROVES ON PRESENT PRACTICES

A number of the aspects of the guidance program are to be found in many classrooms even though they may be referred to by some other title. The implementation of a program of guidance services serves to identify and utilize those activities while providing an opportunity for all pupils in all classrooms to benefit from a similar service. In addition, it may be found that by improved coordination and evaluation certain other services are needed and can be substituted or added for the benefit of all youngsters.

GUIDANCE SERVICES ARE NOT AN ADDED ACTIVITY

Guidance services should not be thought of as an added responsibility but rather as a change in activities. If a change in activities is made, it should be judged by the teacher on this basis: "Will this change make my efforts more meaningful to the youngsters in my room?" Increasing the emphasis upon guidance activities is justifiable only when there is a corresponding increase in the effectiveness of the total educational program of the school.

GUIDANCE SERVICES ARE A GROUP OF FACILITATING SERVICES

Frequently, the guidance program is thought of as something apart from the instructional and administrative functions of the school. As such it would be of doubtful merit. The role that a program of guidance services must play is that of making the instructional and administrative functions more effective through a group of facilitating services.

THE TRAINING BACKGROUND OF GUIDANCE WORKERS PRESUPPOSES CERTAIN ELEMENTS

If the guidance services are to be effective, all staff members should have training in certain areas of preparation. Training in the elementary aspects of the dynamics of human adjustment and individual behavior would seem to be the minimum for all personnel. Introductory courses in child psychology, mental hygiene, sociology, educational psychology, and the guidance services should prove highly desirable as a base for all staff members. Additional training in the specific guidance services should be taken by anyone assigned a specialist's role in the guidance program.

the guidance services

Various authors have suggested several divisions within a program of guidance services. All of the suggestions have merit and usually include similar activities. The differences seem to concern format rather than points of view. To analyze the services that should make up the total program, it is advisable to identify the various obligations of the guidance services to each individual. The following eight obligations are basic:

1. To collect all the significant information about an individual which will be of assistance in furthering his adjustment.
2. To interpret the information to the individual and members of his family whenever such information is needed in order to reach a more objective solution of problems.
3. To furnish to the individual certain kinds of information that is not ordinarily given in the conventional educational

system and which will make his next steps in the learning process more realistic and meaningful.

4. To interpret this information to the individual or his family so that a maximum of benefit from the information can be expected.
5. To assist the individual in a complete analysis of all factors which are associated with his adjustment to his environment.
6. To alter the environment of the individual, whenever possible, so as to increase the speed and effectiveness of his adjustment.
7. To aid the individual in adjusting to his post-school situation.
8. To follow up the individual after he leaves the school in order to evaluate his post-school adjustment and to obtain information which can be used to alter and improve the school environment.

To meet these obligations, the following services to pupils seem most desirable for a program of guidance services.

PUPIL-INVENTORY SERVICE

The Pupil-Inventory Service is concerned with a careful and systematic study of each student in order to personalize his educational program as much as possible. It includes all of the tools and techniques used to obtain significant information about every individual. Questionnaires, autobiographies, sociograms, tests, anecdotes, and the techniques for recording and interpreting the information make up the major part of this aspect of a guidance program.

INFORMATION SERVICE

The Information Service consists of three very closely related phases. The parts are designated by the type of information and are known as the occupational, educational, and personal-social phases. Occupational information is information about the world of work; educational information is information about present and future learning experiences; and personal-social information is that which will be of assistance to the individual in understanding his own behavior and that of his peers.

COUNSELING SERVICE

The Counseling Service provides competent personnel, facilities, and time in order that every pupil can have an opportunity to discuss his concerns on an individual basis. Because it is based on the theory that the counseling process is an individualized activity, this service does not include various group processes sometimes referred to as group counseling.

PLACEMENT SERVICE

The Placement Service is an integral service of the total guidance program. The main purpose of this service is to aid the individual in making a good adjustment to his post-school experiences. This is achieved through both educational and vocational placement.

FOLLOW-UP AND EVALUATION SERVICE

The Follow-up and Evaluation Service is concerned with the problems, successes, failures, and suggestions of the students after they are in a new situation and have an opportunity to test their educational experiences in the secondary school. A continuous follow-up of school leavers and graduates provides the school staff with information for the improvement of the educational offering of the school.

summary

In this unit it has been pointed out that secondary schools in the United States have dedicated themselves to the task of helping students attain the broad objectives of civic responsibility, economic efficiency, human relationships and self-realization. A guidance program has been defined as a coordinated group of services established within our schools to help pupils reach their maximum potential as individual human beings. They are those services that help children obtain the most from their school experiences through a better understanding of themselves and their environment. They include the pupil-inventory, information, counseling, placement, and follow-up and evaluation services.

It has been emphasized that trained counselors are not the only personnel who provide these guidance services for students. Every staff member shares the responsibility for developing and maintaining the guidance program. Trained counselors are expected to provide leadership, but the classroom teacher is the primary person in the program since he is the one who has the greatest amount of direct contact with students. Administrators also have an important part to play in the planning and perpetuation of a program of guidance services. It is with this thought in mind that the term *guidance worker* is used throughout the remainder of this book to refer to any staff member providing guidance services to students on either a primary or incidental basis.

selected readings

Barry, Ruth and Wolf, Beverly. *Modern Issues in Guidance-Personnel Work.* New York: Teachers College, Columbia University, 1957.

Cottingham, Harold F. *Guidance in the Junior High School.* Bloomington, Illinois: McKnight and McKnight Publishing Company, 1961.

Crow, Lester D. and Crow, Alice. *Readings in Guidance.* New York: David McKay Company, Inc., 1962.

Farwell, Gail F. and Peters, Herman J. *Guidance Readings for Counselors.* Chicago: Rand McNally and Company, 1960.

Froehlich, Clifford P. *Guidance Services in Schools.* New York: McGraw-Hill Book Company, Inc., 1958.

Humphreys, J. Anthony, Traxler, Arthur E., and North, Robert D. *Guidance Services.* Chicago: Science Research Associates, Inc., 1960.

Hutson, Percival W. *The Guidance Function in Education.* New York: Appleton-Century-Crofts, Inc., 1958.

Johnson, Mauritz, Jr., Busacker, William E., and Bowman, Fred Q., Jr. *Junior High School Guidance.* New York: Harper and Brothers Publishers, 1961.

Johnson, Walter F., Stefflre, Buford, and Edelfelt, Roy A. *Pupil Personnel and Guidance Services.* New York: McGraw-Hill Book Company, Inc., 1961.

Miller, Carroll H. *Foundations of Guidance.* New York: Harper and Brothers, Publishers, 1961.

McDaniel, Henry B., Lallas, John E., Saum, James A., and Gilmore, James G. *Readings in Guidance.* New York: Henry Holt and Company, 1959.

Peters, Herman J. and Farwell, Gail F. *Guidance: A Developmental Approach.* Chicago: Rand McNally and Company, 1959.

Rosecrance, Francis C. and Hayden, Velma D. *School Guidance and Personnel Services.* Boston: Allyn and Bacon, Inc., 1960.

Wrenn, C. Gilbert. *The Counselor in a Changing World.* Washington, D. C.: The Commission on Guidance in American Schools, American Personnel and Guidance Association, 1962.

Unit 2

The Pupil-Inventory Service

Methods of Collecting Pupil Information

The pupil-inventory service is concerned with the collection and interpretation of information about individual students. The organization of information requires both an appraisal of its significance and a filing plan which facilitates its use and interpretation. The pupil-inventory service provides the basis for knowing and understanding students as individuals, and thus it must be regarded as an important service in the development of the high school guidance program. This service can be divided into two rather distinct parts, the first being that of collecting information about students, and the second involving the recording and interpretation of such data. This unit will be concerned with the methods of collecting personal data. The following unit will describe procedures for recording and interpreting information of that nature.

some basic criteria for the collection of information[1]

Certain fundamental criteria underlie the collection of meaningful information about pupils. The school staff, interested in developing a good pupil-inventory service, should take cognizance of the factors which determine the value of pupil information. The data should be:

---

[1]Raymond N. Hatch and James W. Costar. *Guidance Services in the Elementary School.* Dubuque, Iowa: Wm. C. Brown Company Publishers, 1961, pp. 45-46.

OBJECTIVE

It a primary goal in the collection of the information about pupils is to increase objectivity, the data will be of greater value. Much of the information that is currently being gathered is too subjective, and unless there is an ever-present awareness of the need to be objective, any information obtained may be too general to be of any great value.

DISTINCTIVE

Much information may be gathered which is similar for every individual in that particular age group. Such data tends to belabor the process and to fill the record with information of no distinct value. To make the information about an individual more useful, data should tend to distinguish that individual as an individual different from his peers.

CUMULATIVE

The amount of information about an individual should be increased by successive additions of new data. This makes it easier to identify the cycles of growth through which an individual has passed and to recognize significant episodes in his development.

areas of essential information

A systematic approach to the collection of information requires that the specific kinds of useful information be identified early. This is a prerequisite to the act of collecting such information which might otherwise be abundant but useless. The following outline includes the major catagories of information found helpful to teachers and counselors with some of the more common specific items in each area.

1. Personal data
   - 1.1 Name, nicknames, picture (age and date), home address
   - 1.2 Sex, birthplace, and date of birth
   - 1.3 Brothers, sisters, and their ages
   - 1.5 Social and economic status
   - 1.6 Religious affiliation and interests (church and related organization memberships)
2. School history
   - 2.1 Schools attended, dates, and grades

   2.2 Courses taken and marks received
   2.3 Attendance record (relation of absences to health, travel, and other problems)
3. Health data
   3.1 Physical (illness, handicaps, deviations from the normal)
   3.2 Mental (traumatic experiences, anxieties)
4. Measured aptitudes and personality traits.
   4.1 Mental abilities (intelligence, verbal and quantitative reasoning)
   4.2 Achievement (mathematics, science, English, basic study skills)
   4.3 Special aptitudes (clerical, mechanical, artistic, musical)
   4.4 Measured interests (vocational, academic, recreational and social activities)
   4.5 Attitudes (values, atypical viewpoints, motivation)
   4.6 Personal and social adjustment (self-understanding, role in groups)
5. Nonacademic experiences
   5.1 Cocurricular (student group affiliations, athletic participation, dramatics, forensics)
   5.2 Community (Boy Scouts, Y.M.C.A. or Y.W.C.A.)
   5.3 Work (summer, school year, full or part-time, nature of work, employer, reaction to work)
   5.4 Travel (time spent, places visited, auspices under which travel took place)
6. Interests and plans
   6.1 Stated interests (vocational, avocational, social, academic)
   6.2 Hobbies and recreational activity (stamp collecting, photography, woodworking)
   6.3 Vocational and life plans (vocational under consideration and reasons, aspirations in regard to a family, place of residence)

It is apparent that the collection of this varied information must involve a wide variety of techniques. At the secondary school level, much of the personal data can be obtained from previous school records or, if appropriate, directly from the student. The child's school history is usually a matter of record. Health data may be available, but, as with certain items in the first category, will need to be brought up to date. Certain items in the remaining three categories are much more subject to change than some of the earlier ones, and recent information will be necessary no matter how complete the earlier records may be.

The various procedures for collecting information can be conveniently divided into three broad areas:

1. Relatively unstructured techniques
2. Personal documents
3. Tests and other highly structured techniques

Each technique in these areas has certain inherent advantages and disadvantages which, to a considerable extent, are characteristic of all techniques in that category. Therefore, these headings comprise a meaningful set for discussion of such procedures.

relatively unstructured techniques

OBSERVATION AS A TOOL FOR GUIDANCE

Actual observations of students as they go about their normal activities is an excellent way of obtaining evidence of behavior in specific situations. A good observation must have some relevance to educational objectives, and it should report actual behavior rather than judgments, interpretations, or recommendations. Observational reports should be behavioral facts rather than inferences. For example, if David and Julie turn in identical arithmetic papers, the statement, "David copied from Julie," is an inference even if Julie is by far the better student. The observation would be, "David turned in an arithmetic paper identical to that of Julie." A similar observation could be made for Julie. On the other hand, if David were under observation while copying, the statement that David copied from Julie is clearly an observation.

It is necessary to keep in mind that single observations have little value. Only as observations are reported on an individual over a period of time in a variety of situations does it become possible to assess their significance. This cumulative requirement is a *must* because there are so many difficulties inherent in the collection of reliable observations. The David-Julie situation illustrates the point. It might be unwise to record the observation, "David turned in an arithmetic paper identical to that of Julie," because this isolated observation may lead to an incorrect perception of David's character.

Once the observation is recorded, many who consult the record will make an unwarranted inference. Recording the observation, "David copied from Julie," is less worrisome; for presumably fact rather than inference is involved. If no similar observations are recorded, this one stands out as reporting what is apparently a typical behavior on David's part and hence possibly involves a clue as to unusual pressures in that particular situation.

One source of difficulty in using observations is the problem of communication. Finding the precise words to convey to others exactly what one has observed requires a careful choice of words from one's own vocabulary in order to avoid those which might have a different meaning for others. "David was sober" might refer equally to absence of joviality or freedom from the effects of alcohol.

Bias or selectivity is a second major difficulty. An observer may note only those reactions consistent with an already established favorable estimate of a person (the so-called halo effect) or observations may be generally unfavorable because of prejudice. In some cases an overly-solicitous teacher concerned about the welfare of a student will unconsciously refrain from noting undesirable behavior. Time also can influence selectivity. It is important that the observations be recorded immediately. Waiting any length of time before writing the report of the incident increases the likelihood that some aspects will be either distorted or completely forgotten.

A third difficulty lies in the rather narrow range of situations which usually come under observation. This increases the possibility that the situations may not provide a true cross section of the child's behavior. Most teachers have felt the surprise that comes when a student who is rather incompetent in the classroom is found to be self-assured and highly competent at some task unrelated to classroom activity or when a good student is found to be incompetent in social situations.

Finally, it is often very difficult to interpret behavior. Just as the same words may have different meanings, the same physical act may be performed for different reasons. In an attempt to overcome this and other difficulties inherent in observations, several different types of observation techniques have been developed. The two most often used are the anecdotal record and the time-sampling chart.

THE TIME-SAMPLING CHART

Time-sampling procedures involve the assignment of a predetermined period of time in which an individual is to be observed. An attempt is made to note rather completely all significant behavior during this time. In this manner the effect of bias or prejudice on selectivity in observation will be minimized. A time sampling of student behavior for an individual known to be singularly unproductive during study periods might appears as follows:

10:15-10:19 Hastily leafed through two books and a notebook as if trying to find assignments and to decide which to do. Finally opened algebra book to a set of problems.

10:19-10:22 Wrote name on paper and started first problem. Decided to sharpen pencil.

10:22-10:30 Returned to desk, stared at wall, doodled on paper, wadded it up, and walked up to throw it in waste basket.

10:30-10:33 Started on new sheet of paper with first problem. Stopped work to watch another student walk to study hall proctor and continued to watch until student returned to seat.

Such a record is helpful not only in clarifying the student's lack of productivity, but it is also valuable information which may help the student understand and change his behavior. However, so much of behavior is apt to be rather routine and uninformative that prolonged time sampling, as a general practice, is not economical. The preceding example suggests that time sampling in the school situation may be most helpful when it is aimed at a problem already identified.

THE ANECDOTAL RECORD

Anecdotal records, involving the firsthand reporting in concise and informal language of significant behavior, both good and bad, represent another observational technique. The procedure can be made simple enough so that a large number of incidents will be obtained from teachers on all students. Usually there is space for interpretations, but it is important that the interpretation be separated from the description of behavior. In theory, anecdotal reports are excellent; in practice, too few are obtained and most of these emphasize negative behavior. Only an unusually observant and guidance-conscious staff of teachers can successfully use this technique. The following anecdotes are examples that provide a basis for specific comments on the problem of writing anecdotes.

Anecdote No. 1

Harry Sundwill Fri. P. M., Jan. 14, 1961

Harry suggested the idea of pupil-supervised study halls. He thought that it would develop responsibility. This shows, for the first time, the reason why he has been such a problem case.

Anecdote No. 2

Student Ted Fay *Date* Feb. 1, 1961

Episode: On the return trip from the Clifton game, Ted told me that he would like to have dates but didn't want to be forced into marriage.

Interpretation: I think someone has given him misinformation on boy-girl relationships.

Action & *Suggestions*: I suggested that he ask Mr. Simmons (the counselor) for a booklet on boy-girl relations.

Bill Pruitt, Coach

The first of these anecdotes was reported on a blank 3 x 5 card. The actual incident — the statement made by the student — is included with the interpretation and thereby loses some of its significance. The statement beginning "He thought . . ." involves an idea not clearly attributed to Harry. It conceivably may be an inference of the reporter, particularly since the next sentence involves an interpretation related to a chain of thought perhaps clear to the reporter but lost to the reader. While it should be kept in mind that anecdotes might include supplementary material which helps to clarify each episode, it is desirable to make the actual description of the behavior reasonably complete in itself.

The second anecdote was written on a prepared form which can be printed on a 4 x 6 or 5 1/2 x 8 1/2 card. It clearly separates the behavior or episode, the interpretation of the reporter, and the action suggested. The second anecdote shows these distinctions, and it has become the basis for a referral to the counselor.

VALUES AND LIMITATIONS OF THE ANECDOTAL RECORD

Broadly speaking, the anecdotal record has considerable value as a guidance technique, but also a number of recognized limitations. It is valuable because (1) students can be studied under conditions which are natural rather than artificial; (2) all age levels can be studied; (3) no special equipment is required; (4) the effects of environmental changes on the student can be studied; (5) the process of writing anecdotes tends to force the attention of the teacher on individual differences in children; and (6) a developmental record can be created over a period of years on the basis of individual anecdotes.[2]

The chief limitations of the anecdotal record exist because (1) any observation is only as valid as the objectivity of the reporter; (2) inexperienced writers of anecdotes may use them to point up undesirable behavior; (3) the writing of anecdotes takes valuable teacher time; and (4) some types of behavior do not lend themselves to observation.[3]

IMPROVING ANECDOTAL RECORDS

To overcome the objections to anecdotal reporting, some basic considerations must be reviewed and accepted by those who are involved in the writing of such reports. The following considerations seem fundamental to a program of anecdotal reporting:

1. The form used for the anecdote should be short and informal yet provide space for the pertinent information.
2. The reports should be of significant episodes. The decision as to what is significant is subjective at best. It may help the observer to make such a decision if the episode is compared with a normal behavior of the individual and of his peer group. If the incident shows a marked tendency from the norm of the individual or group, it is probably significant.
3. Both complimentary and uncomplimentary incidents should be recorded.
4. Anecdotes should be written about all students. There is a marked tendency to report incidents involving those in-

---

[2]*The Anecdotal Record,* Revised Edition, Guidance Staff, East Lansing, Michigan: College of Education, Michigan State University, 1957, pp. 5-6.
[3]Ibid., p. 6.

dividuals found at the upper and lower levels of a given criterion. For example, teachers have a tendency to report incidents involving the brightest and least bright students and disregard the large group to be found between the two extremes.

5. The anecdote should be the report of the actual observer and written very soon after the occurrence of the episode. If the incident is described by a third person or if considerable time elapses before the recording is made, objectivity is reduced.
6. The form of the anecdote should include one space for reporting the literal incident and another for the reporter's interpretation of cause and effect or suggestions. This helps to reduce the common problem of confusing the actual incident with the reporter's opinion of what happened.
7. The anecdote in itself is of little value. It is when several anecdotes from several reports have been collected that the information takes on its most meaningful aspects. Even when the record is quite complete the information should be studied and interpreted with other information gained from other sources.[4]

In general, emphasis on observational techniques has real value in making teachers conscious of students as distinctive individuals, but the problems of collecting and interpreting unbiased and representative samples of behavior make it a technique to be used with caution and only in conjunction with a wide variety of additional sources of information. When the total number of anecdotes reported is small, the odds are that they represent a biased sample of the behavior of students reported upon. As the number of anecdotes increases they are more likely to represent a more typical cross section of student behavior.

personal documents

Personal documents refer here to relatively unstructured statements written by the student, describing or interpreting his experiences. The *autobiography* covers his entire life to the time of writing with some projection of his plans for the future. It is

[4]Raymond N. Hatch. *The Anecdotal Record,* East Lansing, Michigan: College of Education, Michigan State University, 1950, p. 3.

something of an historical summary of presently recalled and presumably significant experiences in the child's life. The *diary,* the other most common form of personal document, is written more or less concurrently with experience. However, for some students it may involve considerable retrospection as well as introspection.

THE AUTOBIOGRAPHY

Most high school teachers and counselors are well aware of the importance of observation, anecdotal records, and standardized tests in helping them understand students. However, the story of the child's life as he reveals it in writing is often overlooked. The autobiography is a systematic account of his life written by the student. Its uses, values, and limitations have been conveniently summarized in the pamphlet, *The Autobiography,* prepared by the counselor education staff at Michigan State University.[5]

Uses of the Autobiography

1. It is valuable in getting the over-all picture of the important events in the child's life.
2. It offers subjective information about the child's likes, dislikes, interests, ambitions, desires and concerns.
3. It offers an opportunity for close inspection of basic personality dynamics at work.
4. It presents personal data about the pupil which can be compared with information from other sources.
5. It promotes self-understanding by encouraging the student to take a close look at himself.

Values of the Autobiography

The autobiography assists the teacher and the student in the following ways:

1. The *teacher* can learn about significant feelings, attitudes, aspirations and experiences of the student.
2. Less *staff* time and effort are required to administer and interpret the autobiography than to secure the same information through an interview.
3. The *student* can gain insight, clarification, or release through describing himself and his past experiences.

---

[5]*The Autobiography,* Guidance Staff, East Lansing, Michigan: College of Education, Michigan State University, 1958, pp. 1-2.

4. The *student* has freedom to discuss the topics *he feels* are important and to avoid those which he fears or holds less important.

Limitations of the Autobiography

1. The information must be verified through other sources of data.
2. Quite often the student's age, intelligence, or background adversely affects his ability to write.
3. If good rapport has not been established, the student may fail to mention pertinent data or may even deliberately distort the facts.

The autobiography demands a high degree of rapport between the student and the person requesting the autobiography. The latter may be the counselor working with the student or, if desirable and appropriate, the English teacher who may regularly require an autobiography as one of the assignments in his course. Usually it is desirable in either case to present the student with an outline of major points to be discussed in the autobiography. The following are elements which might be mentioned:

1. Early history and family background
2. Health and physical record
3. School history
4. Interests, leisure time activities, hobbies, travel experiences, friendships
5. Occupational experiences
6. Educational and vocational plans
7. Desires and plans regarding marriage and a home

The preceding categories of information may need to be rephrased somewhat if they are to be given as a guide to pupils. Some such revision as the following might be appropriate:

1. What personal experiences and events do you recall most vividly from the years before you entered school? What seem to you to be the most interesting and significant facts about your family background?
2. What accidents, illnesses, or disabilities have you experienced which have modified your plans or viewpoints?

3. What schools have you attended? What stands out most strongly in your mind about each? What events, other than promotion, led you to change from one school to another?

Similar modifications of the other categories into questions more suggestive to students can easily be made.

DIRECTIONS FOR WRITING THE AUTOBIOGRAPHY

Autobiographies are often referred to as *structured* or *unstructured* depending upon the kind of directions that are given to the pupil. Highly explicit and detailed directions requesting factual information are typical of the *structured* autobiography. With the *unstructured* autobiography the pupil is given a loose set of directions that may include little more than the request to "Write a story about your life." The *structured* autobiography is an efficient means of acquiring a systematic and detailed account of the child's life. An *unstructured* autobiography is more apt to reveal what the child perceives as the most important areas of information about himself, e.g., his interests, aspirations, joys, and concerns. It is much more difficult to extract from this type the full meaning of the subtle clues regarding just what the child feels, consciously or unconsciously, is an important aspect of his life or personality. In either case, the autobiography must be considered a subjective technique for the collection of information. If the writer's efforts are not directed toward a general framework, the results may be confusing to him and to the reader.[6]

THE DIARY

It is more difficult to get students to maintain a *diary* since this demands continuing attention for some time rather than being an assignment which can be completed within a relatively short period. While some people like to keep diaries, most are not interested. Furthermore, a diary kept on the basis of a request or assignment is likely to be much different in nature than one an individual would keep for his own purposes. In working with individual students it is frequently helpful to request that the student maintain a log of his daily activities over a week or so. This is related to, but rather different from, a diary, in that the emphasis is on obtaining a record of the sequence of activities and the amount

[6]Hatch and Costar, op. cit., p. 43.

of time spent on each. This is particularly helpful when working with a student on study procedures and the related problem of time budgeting. Such records are somewhat like the time-sampling adaptation of observation, but the log of daily activities is self-administered and ordinarily deals with larger blocks of time.

INTERPRETING THE AUTOBIOGRAPHY AND DIARY

All variations of the autobiography and the diary raise certain problems in interpretation. The student's poor vocabulary or his inability to write present definite limitations, particularly in communicating feelings of considerable depth. The student may, even without intending to, be so motivated that his diary or autobiography gives an erroneous portrayal of his life. He may get carried away by sheer delight (perhaps unmerited) in his literary ability. He may see in the task an opportunity for increasing his own self-understanding or developing a basis for receiving assistance from a counselor. In any case, the results can vary considerably according to the motivation; and since the student is often unaware of his motivation, anyone who attempts to interpret his autobiography cannot be certain of it.

Aside from the well-known use of the autobiography to gain insight into the student's life as he sees it, other suggestions have been made for its utilization:

1. Specific facts stated therein can be checked against other sources. Falsifications or poor recollection, revealed by discrepancies, might have significance.
2. Lack of agreement between items of information may suggest further investigation in some cases. Thus an autobiography of a high school pupil revealing an adopted status not previously recorded might be a clue to a recent traumatic experience for that individual.
3. Discontinuities or omissions in the autobiography may be indicative of periods involving unpleasant recollections.
4. The selection of certain words and phrases can reveal a great deal about the pupil's educational and cultural background. Variation in the uses of words or in the style of writing about different phases of experience may be indicative of emotional tension.

These suggestions are to be followed with caution. Certainly any inferences or "hunches" should be checked against other sources of information. In the main, they afford only leads to be utilized by a competent counselor. The untrained individual may, by reaching a quick conclusion, make himself appear ridiculous or do actual harm to the student.

tests and other high structured techniques

Techniques to be discussed in this section differ from those in preceding sections in somewhat the same way that objective tests differ from essay tests. Data blanks and questionnaires are similar to completion tests, and like many of the standardized procedures to be mentioned, are definitely objective. However, objectivity is not the only criterion involved, for the rating scales included in this discussion include subjective responses even though they are highly structured.

PERSONAL DATA BLANKS

Data blanks or questionnaires can be used in conducting a structured or guided interview. Usually it is more economical to attempt to develop such a blank or questionnaire to the point where, after a few simple instructions, a student – or indeed a whole group of students – can complete the blank without additional assistance. To be effective, certain criteria need to be kept in mind when developing the instruments:

1. There should be a definite reason for inclusion of each item – not just curiosity.
2. The information requested should be commonly known. Asking for information not generally known by pupils may create an attitude which will make other responses less valid and raise questions regarding the importance of the information requested.
3. Desired answers should be factual, brief, definite, and highly specific. They should also be impersonal in the sense that all the questions asked are equally applicable to all students even though the answers may be quite different.

The usability of such an instrument is greatly enhanced by arranging the items of information requested so that:

1. The most significant and commonly used items are readily available.

2. The order of the items corresponds to the sequence used in the cumulative record folder.

The following form represents a one-page data sheet of the type that can be helpful to any teacher or counselor preparing for a counseling interview.

PERSONAL DATA SHEET

Name .... Date ....
Last First Middle

Address .... Telephone No. ....

Birthplace .... Date of Birth ....
Father's name .... Mother's name ....
Father's occupation .... Mother's occupation ....
No. of older brothers .... No. of older sisters ....
No. of younger brothers .... No. of younger sisters ....
No. of brothers and sisters now attending this school ....
Names of schools previously attended (list grades completed in each) ....
....
What school subjects do you like best? ....
Why? ....
What subjects do you dislike? ....
Why? ....
What grades, if any, have you repeated? ....
Do you play a musical instrument? .... Which? ....
Do you enjoy reading? .... What kinds of material do you read? ....
....
How often do you attend the movies? ....
What kind of movies do you like? ....
Do you have a radio set at home? .... Television? ....
What programs do you particularly like? ....
....
What special interests or hobbies do you have? ....
....
Do you have a room of your own? .... Radio of your own?.......... TV? ....
What traveling have you done? (Where and how long?) ....
....
Summer camps attended and dates ....
....
Responsibilities or duties at home ....
....
Do you plan to go to college? .... Where? ....
What vocation, if any, have you selected? ....
Why? ....

Such a questionnaire as the one above may be altogether too lacking in detail for some situations. The following section from a nine-page questionnaire indicates the kind of elaboration and detail which can be obtained if desired.

MY LEISURE TIME ACTIVITIES AND INTERESTS

1. The types of magazines and books (mystery, travel, fiction, current events etc.) I enjoy are ....
....
2. I read newspapers:
................every day ....on Sundays only
................occasionally ....almost never
3. The parts of the newspaper I enjoy reading most are:
................comic sections ....woman's page
................the editorials ....society news
................sports section ....general news of the day
4. I enjoy the following types of radio and TV programs:
................news summaries ....quiz programs
................news commentators ....grand opera
................commentators from abroad ....entertainment programs (Jack Benny, Ed Sullivan, Bob Hope)
................soap operas
................classical music or old masters ....symphony concerts
................others (please list):
................dance bands
................mystery dramas
5. My chief forms of amusement are:
........dancing ....card games ....skating and skiing
........swimming ....reading ....hunting
........movies ....golf, tennis, etc. ....fishing
........riding ....others (please list) ....bowling
........hiking
6. I take an active part in or am a member of the following organizations:
........4-H Clubs ....YMCA or YWCA ....basketball team
........Grange ....Literary Club ....football team
........church groups ....Glee Club ....baseball team
........Scouts ....clubs (Latin, math., dramatics, etc.) ....band or orchestra
........others (please list):
7. The number of students in my grade school was approximately ....
8. It has always been possible for me to take part in the activities of school groups. Yes .... No...........
9. I have usually preferred activities engaged in by
................a large group ....a small group
................one particular friend ....my family
................two or three people ....myself alone
10. I have a special hobby. Yes .... No...........
Describe:

It should be observed that the second questionnaire form differs from the first in that it has a larger amount of structuring. More specific items are brought to the attention of the student, thus to some extent overcoming differences in the willingness or ability of students to recall and reveal their activities and interests. Some risks are also involved because the more detailed form can cause some students to feel pressured to check more items in an effort to create the illusion of well rounded development.

Major issues in connection with such information-obtaining devices are apt to arise. One factor which pertains to all such information is the extent to which it is regarded and actually treated as confidential. More will be said concerning this issue in the following unit on records. Another issue is the possible controversial nature of certain items of information. Questions about parents' income, religion, politics, and the like may have significance in understanding an individual student, but can also cause considerable reaction when the policy of collecting them is first initiated. A closely related issue involves the legality of requests for certain kinds of information. In a number of states anti-discrimination legislation forbids the use of certain types of information, such as race or religion, as parts of formal records. Finally, there is the problem of reliability. Some students have only the haziest ideas about the incomes of their fathers but will put down something rather than confess complete ignorance. There must be a constant awareness of such unreliability in using this type of information.

RATING SCALES

A rating scale involves a directed or structured observation usually embracing descriptions of conduct or behavior patterns and providing some means of indicating a judgment with respect to quality, frequency, or importance for each item. Rating scales provide one of the simplest ways to obtain information about personal characteristics either as observed in a single sample of behavior or as summarized over a period of time through repeated contacts. Rating scales quickly reveal these things when they are phrased in terms of such observable characteristics as being on time to class or participating in class discussions.

Rating of an individual student can be done by the teacher, by other students, or by the student himself. Teacher ratings, provided they are collected from a number of teachers in order to increase reliability by combining several judgments, are useful in making reports to parents, college admissions officers, or prospective employers. Ratings made by teachers, peers, or the student can facilitate and encourage self-evaluation.

Various approaches to ratings have been developed. The more common types are:

1. Graphic
2. Descriptive
3. Man-to-man

The *graphic* form of rating scale is one of the simplest to use. It is illustrated in Figure 1 by an example taken from a high school record prepared by a committee of high school principals in Virginia. In this example verbal descriptions have been placed on the scale to give added meaning, but checks can be made at any point. Purely numerical scales are sometimes used, but they are satisfactory only if tangible meaning has been assigned to each number.

The *descriptive* form of rating scale can be combined with the graphic form as just illustrated. However, a purely descriptive technique might be used alone as shown by the example in Figure 2. The number of descriptions can be increased and made much more specific if desired, but the form is likely to be very cumbersome if this is done. Two features of this personality rating scale are worthy of note:

1. Provision for indicating "no adequate opportunity to observe" helps to prevent forcing highly unreliable checking by teachers with little basis for response.
2. The request for specific instances to illustrate or justify the estimate enforces some reflection in checking the personality qualities. In effect, this feature provides for brief anecdotal reports of behavior.

Man-to-man rating involves the comparison of an individual with a known or hypothetical person familiar to the rater. It is probably less well adapted to the school situation than a modified form which involves classifying an entire group of students in regard to a single characteristic. Three or more levels of classification can be used. In using three levels, those students who are outstanding in regard to the characteristic would be assigned to the first class, those considered as average to the second, and those judged as inferior to the third. The preassignment of a percentage to each class may assist the discrimination; for example, 25-50-25 for three classes or 10-20-40-20-10 if five classes are used. Such percentage assignments enforce a limited ranking and a differentiation which some teachers will hesitate to make otherwise.

The acknowledged subjectivity in ratings is their major weakness. Not infrequently, ratings of students reveal as much about the raters as about the students. Haziness and differences in interpretation of the characteristics rated are major elements in this subjectivity. So, too, is the halo effect — the tendency to rate all characteristics in terms of a generally favorable or unfavorable evaluation of an individual. A partial answer to the halo effect is

PERSONAL DATA RECORD	Confidential	TERMINAL EVALUATION	Date	Grade	
Seriousness of Purpose	Not Evidenced	Some	Average	Above Ave.	Purposeful
Industry	Not Evidenced	Needs Pressure	Needs Prodding	Prepares Work	Additional Work
Initiative	Not Evidenced	Initiative	Average	Above Ave.	Very Much
Concern for Others	Anti-Social	Self-Centered	Average	Concerned	Strongly Concerned
Influence on Others	Not Evidenced	Some	Average	Above Ave.	Very Much
Responsibility	Not Evidenced	Some	Usually Dependable	Conscientious	Very
Emotional Stability	Very Emotional	Excitable	Usually Well Balanced	Well Balanced	Very Stable
	Apathetic	Unresponsive			

Figure 1

Personality report of .... Class .... Date ....

Name of Person rated

I have had this person in the following courses ....

1. Does he think clearly and rapidly; has he many ideas? Can he convey his ideas clearly?

- ☐ Is a keen, resourceful, quick thinker.
- ☐ Is a rapid and clear thinker.
- ☐ Is a slow but a clear thinker.
- ☐ Is a slow and unclear thinker.
- ☐ Is a dull and "muddy" thinker.
- I have had no adequate opportunity to observe this trait ☐

Please give here specific instances to illustrate your estimate. What has he done?

2. Is he tolerant of new ideas; is he open minded and receptive to progressive suggestions?

- ☐ Eagerly welcomes ideas and suggestions.
- ☐ Open to ideas and suggestions.
- ☐ Usually openminded.
- ☐ Frequently objects to the new.
- ☐ Objects to and opposes everything new.
- I have had no adequate opportunity to observe this trait ☐

Please give here specific instances to illustrate your estimate. What has he done?

3. Does he get his work done on time?

- ☐ Conscientiously endeavors to finish work promptly and ahead of time.
- ☐ Habitually completes his work on time.
- ☐ Usually completes his work on time.
- ☐ Occasionally late in completion of his work.
- ☐ Nearly always late in completion of his work.
- I have had no adequate opportunity to observe this trait ☐

Please give here specific instances to illustrate your estimate. What has he done?

4. Does he do more than he is told or must he be continually prodded?

- ☐ Does "twice as much as he is told."
- ☐ Seeks and creates additional tasks for himself.
- ☐ Does additional assignments upon suggestion only.
- ☐ Creates new tasks for himself only under pressure.
- ☐ Never does anything unless he is told.
- I have had no adequate opportunity to observe this trait. ☐

Please give here specific instances to illustrate your estimate. What has he done?

5. Is he ambitious or is he easily satisfied with low attainment?

- ☐ Absorbed in attaining his ambitions.
- ☐ Eager to achieve his ambitions.
- ☐ Occasionally ambitious.
- ☐ Aims just "to get by."
- ☐ Has no ambition.
- I have had no adequate opportunity to observe this trait ☐

Please give here specific instances to illustrate your estimate. What has he done?

6. Can he be depended upon to carry out obligations or is he unreliable and irresponsible?

- ☐ Scrupulously fulfills obligations.
- ☐ Habitually willing and responsible.
- ☐ Usually fulfills obligations.
- ☐ Fulfills obligations when convenient.
- ☐ Constantly neglects all obligations.
- I have had no adequate opportunity to observe this trait ☐

Please give here specific instances to illustrate your estimate. What has he done?

Figure 2

7. How well does he control his emotions?

- ☐ Unusually well-balanced and controlled.
- ☐ Well-balanced.
- ☐ Usually well-balanced.
- ☐ Occasionally over-emotional.
- ☐ Easily moved to tears, fits of depression or anger.
- I have had no adequate opportunity to observe this trait ☐

Please give here specific instances to illustrate your estimate. What has he done?

8. Does he get others to accept his plans and purposes and carry them out?

- ☐ Arouses an enthusiastic following; a born leader.
- ☐ Secures cooperation of most of his group.
- ☐ Occasionally takes the lead.
- ☐ Satisfied to let others take the lead.
- ☐ Never wins group support; creates antagonisms.
- I have had no adequate opportunity to observe this trait ☐

Please give here specific instances to illustrate your estimate. What has he done?

9. What deficiencies of general character and personality should he attempt to remedy?

Please record here any physical deficiencies.

10. How good is he in his preparation, skill, insight and ability in the subject matter of

....

(Fill in name of subject)

- ☐ Is a genius in this field; it would be a great mistake for him not to exploit his superior talent by specializing.
- ☐ Ranks among the pupils of excellent promise in this field.
- ☐ Is of only fair promise in this field.
- ☐ Is of poor promise. Not advisable to continue.
- ☐ Has a special disability; it seems impossible for him to make progress.
- I have had no adequate opportunity to observe this trait ☐

Please give here specific instances to illustrate your estimate. What has he done?

From your knowledge of this person, in what occupation or occupations do you think he would do best? ....

In what activities outside of the classroom have you observed him to excel? ....

What intellectual interests, outside of the required school work, has he displayed? ....

In light of all the above, would you advise him to go to college? ....

(Please give the reason for your answer.)

....

Have you ever discussed this person's future with his parents? ....

Have you ever had a talk with this person about his occupation? ....

If so, with what results? ....

How well do you know this person?—
- ☐ Intimately
- ☐ From childhood
- ☐ Few years
- ☐ Short time
- ☐ In classes only

Signature ....

Title (or position) ....

Subjects taught by you ....

Ohio College Association Rating Scale. Form O.

Figure 2 (Continued)

found in varying the order of the descriptions or of the graphs so that the desirable rating is not always at the same location. This forces the rater to exercise greater care, but can also introduce errors by rapid raters and generally makes the rating an even more unpleasant task. The most obvious caution is to use all ratings with care, checking them whenever possible against other sources of information.

THE ROLE OF STANDARDIZED TESTS[7]

At one stage in the early development of the field of guidance a testing program was frequently thought of as *the* guidance program. Gradually, testing has been relegated to a less important role until today it is considered only one of the many methods of collecting information about pupils. When one remembers that the collection of pupil information is but a part of one of the five major guidance services, it can be readily seen that testing is a small aspect of the total program of guidance services. In spite of this fact, the contribution made by standardized tests is a significant and necessary part of the operation of a successful guidance program.

The exact role of standardized testing in the secondary school has been a point of some contention for several decades. Few authors in the field of guidance have identified the role of tests in the secondary school but speak of testing in the entire school system. Generally speaking, standardized tests serve the same broad purpose in the high school as they do at any other level, namely, to provide teachers and students with knowledge that is helpful to them in planning and selecting appropriate learning experiences. However, the nature of these tasks at this level is such that information concerning the child's native ability to acquire knowledge and his skill in the use of the basic tools of learning is the most valuable. For this reason tests of intelligence, interests, and achievement constitute the major part of most testing programs in secondary schools. Personality tests assume a minor role and are used most often with special cases, if at all.

Writers in the area of educational measurement usually suggest tests of intelligence, interest, aptitude, and achievement for use at the secondary school level. The reader may have noted writings

[7]The next three sections of this unit have been adapted from Raymond N. Hatch and James W. Costar. *Guidance Services in the Elementary School.* Dubuque, Iowa: William C. Brown Company, Publishers, 1961, pp. 73-75.

which referred to tests of intelligence as a type of aptitude test and grouped diagnostic and achievement tests into one category. The various points of view have resulted in some confusion for the user of tests in guidance work. It would seem that the choice of certain areas of testing in the secondary school should be predicated on one major criterion, that of the need for a certain kind of information to aid in the adjustment of the pupil. If such a criterion is applied, the use of tests both for measurement of mental ability and for diagnosis are basic to understanding an individual. Tests of special aptitude may have a role, but present instruments are probably not sufficiently refined to be of much assistance to the guidance worker in the secondary school.

The field of testing is a professional field in itself. It includes the construction of test items and their compilation into tests. It covers the method of arriving at normative data and how to interpret that data. Many volumes have been written which describe this work in detail. All such information is extremely helpful to the guidance worker, but the primary concern of the classroom teacher is the interpretation of the data. It is toward this end that the following material has been written. If the reader wishes further information, there are now available many excellent textbooks dealing with standardized tests. A few of the more appropriate ones are listed at the end of this chapter.

WHAT IS MEASURED?

Of the many techniques used in the collection of information about students mentioned thus far, tests are the most objective. Yet in spite of this objectivity, faulty interpretation of test results has led to much misunderstanding and misinformation. The tendency of staff members to "read into" a test score more than one should expect occurs all too frequently. The guidance worker has the obligation to interpret test information within the limits of its demonstrated usefulness and to help all staff members see the information in a similar light.

Publishers of standardized tests usually provide guidance workers with a manual of directions for test administration and interpretation. The administrative directions are ordinarily quite understandable, but frequently the material describing the significance of the test scores utilizes terms which are easily misinterpreted by the test user. The meanings of certain norms provide excellent examples of factors which may be misunderstood. Most test manuals offer tables of norms so that the test user can convert the raw scores made on the test to a norm for comparative interpretation. Interpreting the norms in the proper manner is the most important aspect of the entire process of measurement. Recognition of the particular significance of a given norm tends to prevent improper interpretation of test results. Raw test scores in the secondary school usually are converted to one or more of the following norms: (1) age norm, (2) grade norm, (3) percentile norm, (4) the intelligence quotient, or (5) mental age. The age norm is the assigned value, in terms of chronological years, which represents an average performance for pupils of a given age. The grade norm is a value for average performance on a standardized test by pupils in a given grade. To understand percentile norms, it is necessary to identify the meaning of percentiles. When a distribution of scores is divided into one hundred parts, each part is referred to as a percentile. The percentile norm is then a value representing percentile ranks of scores on standardized tests for certain subjects. The fourth common type of norm is the I. Q. which is the ratio between mental age and chronological age. The mental age is the mental ability of a particular child expressed in terms of the chronological age for which his mental ability is typical. Interpretation of test results implies an obligation to use the norms within their limits, each one having a particular significance to the test user.

ADMINISTERING STANDARDIZED TESTS

Carefully selected and scheduled standardized tests are essential to a good testing program, but it is equally important to have the tests carefully administered. No amount of cautious planning can make the testing program worthwhile if the test results for each pupil are not valid measures of the child's ability to perform the tasks that are included in the examinations. The fact that the exercise is called a standardized test suggests that there are standard procedures for administering and scoring them. Before the examiner can compare the performance of a student in his school with the performance of the students used in establishing the test norms, the conditions under which the test is given must be essentially the same. Therefore, it is extremely important for the person administering a standardized test, first of all, to become familiar with the contents of the test manual furnished by the publishers of the test. The validity of the results will be further increased if the examiner will follow the suggestions listed here:

1. Take the test yourself before giving it to the pupils.
2. Do not "coach" pupils who are to take a particular test.
3. Be prepared to hand out all the materials that are necessary quickly so that the natural enthusiasm for taking a test will not be lost in unnecessary confusion.
4. Try to administer the test under the ordinary classroom conditions to which the pupils are accustomed.
5. Increase the pupils' motivation for taking the test by letting them know why they are taking the test and exactly how the results are to be used.
6. Follow the directions for administering the test exactly but in a manner that is friendly and relaxed.
7. Where time limits are specified, try to observe them to the fraction of a second.
8. Note any unusual circumstances which may have affected the performance of any of the pupils.
9. Wherever the tests are scored by machine or someone else, it is a good idea to make sure that it has been done accurately by rescoring a sample of the tests.
10. Under certain circumstances it might be advisable to protect the identity of the pupils by assigning them code numbers to be placed on the examinations instead of their names.

Information gathered about pupils through the use of standardized tests is of little value unless it is used properly. Those aspects of the pupil-inventory service related to the recording and interpretation of this and other types of pupil data are discussed in the following unit.

INTERPRETING STANDARDIZED TEST SCORES

In situations where a standardized test is given to an entire class, it may be sufficient to use a scoring and reporting scheme which compares an individual with others in his group. Raw scores – involving the number of right answers or the number of right less some proportion of the wrong answers – do not make meaningful comparisons possible. Percentile scores which show a person's relative position in a group by indicating the per cent of the group which he surpasses facilitate comparison. Another means of comparison is the use of transformed scores with 50 as the mean and 10 as the standard deviation. These scores put individual scores in a form which indicates the position of the person above or below the group average (arithmetic mean) in terms of the variation (standard deviation) in the group. For those familiar wth them, these transformed or standard scores are more useful than percentiles, although the computation – for the novice – is more difficult.

For many purposes local norms affording comparability only within a limited group are entirely unsatisfactory. For example, in reading ability it may be that the local group is atypical and it is therefore desirable to have available norms based upon some more extensive (state or national) population. If mechanical ability is being tested and the results are to be used in vocational guidance, it is desirable to have available data not only comparing the individual with other students but also with appropriate occupational groups. The availability of such norms or standards, accompanied by evidence of reliability and validity, is a characteristic of standardized tests.

The preceding remarks are quite inadequate to convey the many issues involved in selecting and interpreting standardized tests, but they should indicate that the kind of data available on a test is an important consideration. Other factors to be reviewed in selecting tests include the ease of administration and scoring, the time required, and the cost. Tests which can be given during a regular school period are much easier to use than ones with longer time intervals. A distinction should be made here between tests to be administered to all students and those which will be used only with individual students in counseling. Individual testing can utilize many instruments not so readily used with large groups.

Every school should have a carefully planned testing program. The extent of the program will vary a great deal, depending on the resources of the school. The point in time at which tests are administered will depend upon circumstances within the school and within the total system. Extensive testing in the ninth grade would make certain kinds of testing unnecessary in the tenth grade. Obviously, a good testing program involves too many factors for one to recommend certain tests without knowing a great deal about the entire school system. Hence, the remarks to follow will consider kinds of information which are useful rather than specific tests.

WHY HAVE A TESTING PROGRAM?[8]

For development of a good testing program the proper purposes of testing must be considered. Four major purposes have been identified as basic.

1. Tests can be given to *improve the instructional program* The school's prime reason for gathering information about students is to aid the teacher in planning the work of the class and in evaluating teaching. This purpose will be fulfilled only if the teacher believes in differentiating instruction. If he believes that he will need to vary his materials, techniques, and goals in keeping with the nature of the child, then a testing program can be most helpful. If, however, his belief is that he should teach the same things in the same way with the same materials regardless of the ability and achievement of the children, then nothing is achieved by providing him with information about children.
2. Tests can be given to *facilitate curriculum revision.* By learning the ability and achievement levels of the students, curriculum planners can make wiser judgments regarding the scope and the sequence of learning experiences which are to be offered to various groups of children. Results of a testing program alone are not a sufficient basis for curriculum revision. No test expert will be sufficiently acquainted with a particular local situation to build a test which will properly measure all the objectives of that school system.
3. Tests provide information for *educational and vocational counseling.* This purpose needs little stressing, since too often the testing program has been totally associated with counseling at the expense of instruction and administration. This purpose is legitimate and important, but is by no means the only reason for giving tests.
4. Tests can be given to help the administrative staff *appraise the educational program.* Testing is not by itself an evalua-

[8]*Let's Look at Our Testing Program,* Guidance Staff, East Lansing, Michigan: College of Education, Michigan State University, 1959, p. 3.

tion. Tests can supply some information which, when added to other information, may permit a realistic judgment of the extent to which the total school is fulfilling its educational purposes. Tests should never be used, however, to evaluate teaching effectiveness of staff.

These four purposes must be clarified before a testing program can be properly developed. Many testing programs have been unsuccessful because the purposes were not made clear.

HOW IS A TESTING PROGRAM DEVELOPED?[9]

A three-step process of development is likely to be most workable. *What information is needed? Who will use the information? How will it be used?*

1. The first step is to formulate clearly *what* information is needed and desired. This step is probably best taken by a staff committee representing instruction, personnel, curriculum, and administration. A group such as this may decide that the teacher at the fifth-grade level should know the spelling achievement of the class; that the counselor at the twelfth-grade level should know the students' vocational interests; etc. When they have described in detail the information they need at the various grade levels, the first step is completed.
2. The second step is to specify *who* will use the information. It is possible that an intelligence test may provide the administrator with an over-all judgment about the nature of the school population. At the same time, the intelligence tests may provide the curriculum specialist with hints as to the kind of program which would be most appropriate. The counselor may use the same test, which, when interpreted to the child and his parent, will be useful in making a vocational decision. Finally, the test data will be useful to the teacher in selecting materials and methods appropriate for the individual child.
3. The third step is to designate specifically *how* the information will be used. Will other texts be used with the children who deviate from the class average in reading ability? Will

---

[9]Ibid., p. 4.

the counselor provide scholarship information to students of high ability? It is unwise to proceed with a testing program which offers only vague hope that somehow the obtained information will be used to the advantage of the child.

SOCIOMETRIC TESTING

The discussion thus far has centered around standardized tests which are usually developed and printed by test publishing companies. There are, however, circumstances when it is more appropriate for the classroom teacher to devise his own less standardized instruments. Tests of this type are most often used by a teacher to measure the academic achievement of his students. Another common practice of teachers is to develop sociometric tests for acquiring information concerning personal and social interaction among students.

Much information can be obtained from the results of sociometric testing. The following examples illustrate the various types of information revealed in the presentation of sociometric data:

The Leaders. Those pupils who are recognized by their classmates as the ones to whom they would be most apt to turn for leadership and assistance in a given situation.

The Isolates. Those individuals who are not selected by any other members of the group as friends or people with whom they would like to work.

The Mutual Choices. Those individuals who may not be integrated into the group but who depend upon each other as demonstrated by reciprocal choices.

The Cliques. Three or more individuals who are isolated from the rest of the group because they have selected each other.

The Rejectees. Those individuals who are rejected by certain members of the group. They can be identified if negative choices are asked for on the questionnaire.[10]

The increasing awareness of guidance workers of the importance of the interaction of an individual with other individuals has led to great interest in techniques indicative of the reactions of a student to his associates and of his associates to him. This widely used technique is relatively simple, involving essentially a request that students indicate by name their first, second, and third choice of fellow students with whom they would like to work, from whom

---

[10]Hatch and Costar, op. cit., p. 65.

they would like scholastic assistance, with whom they would like to sit, or some other equally immediate and relevant choice. There is considerable disagreement as to the advisability of asking the students to similarly indicate their dislikes, but there is no doubt that the additional information is highly significant. A simple chart can be constructed to show the pattern of choices and rejections for each individual.

The following question indicates the relatively simple way in which the basic sociometric data are obtained. In this case the use of the questionnaire is a prelude to organizing the class into a number of small working committees.

List three other students in the class with whom you would like to work on the homecoming committee to decorate the auditorium.

1. ______________________
2. ______________________
3. ______________________

The following tabulation sheet shows how the data accruing from the answers to this question can be organized. Each student is given a number, and this number is placed after the name of the student he has chosen. For example, Davenport was chosen by number 6, Gerst.

TABULATION SHEET*

Student	Chosen by
1. Davenport	6
2. Dove	15
3. Failen	2-5-9
4. Foster	(15)-(8)
5. Gainor	4
6. Gerst	10
7. Hackett	14
8. Hess	(4)-(14)
9. Hyle	1-6-7-8-11-12-13-14
10. Innis	4
11. Joyce	4
12. Kell	6-13
13. Mentzer	5
14. More	3-(8)-10-(15)
15. Nott	(4)-(14)

*Numbers in parentheses indicate mutual choices.

Several facts become more distinguishable on the tabulation sheet. Not all students made three selections, since the total number of choices is thirty-one rather than the expected forty-five. Every

Sociogram

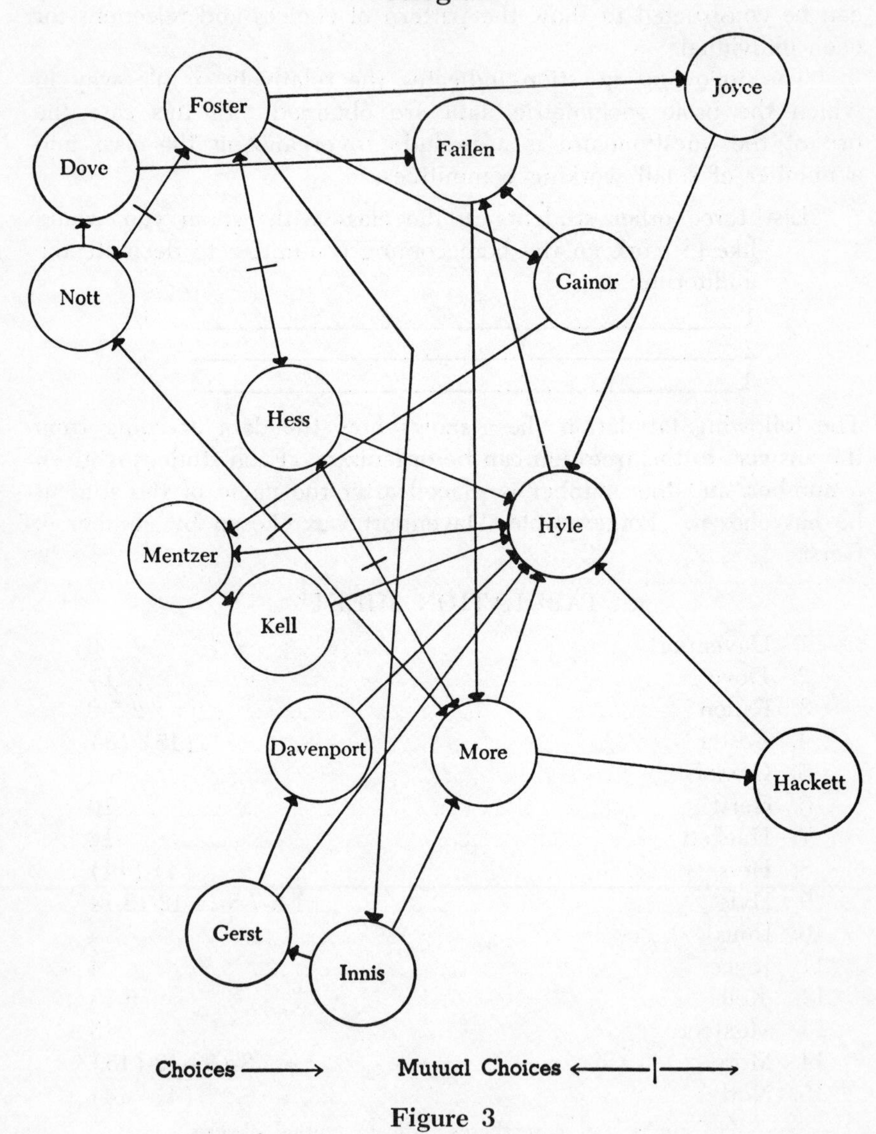

Figure 3

student was selected at least once. Hyle stands out from the group with a total of eight selections, none of which were reciprocal. In addition, the preceding graphic portrayal shown makes it somewhat easier to see the specific relationships involved.

The clusters of choices, the mutual choices, and the near isolates can be detected by a glance at this chart. It should be kept in mind, however, that the ties indicated hold only for the question posed and might be quite different were the question aimed at some other area of activity.

The sociometric approach can be made much more elaborate than the situation which has just been illustrated. Ranking the students who are named or indicating the preferred one for chairman would inject a somewhat higher degree of discrimination. Presentation of additional questions involving selections on other bases and perhaps camouflaged by insertion of additional nonsociometric questions would widen the range of interrelationships studied.

This technique has considerable value in identifying "in groups" and rejected individuals. The major difficulties lie in limiting the results to the immediate situation and in interpreting the variation from day to day in the judgments that are made. Despite these limitations, the data gathered by this means can be very helpful to the teacher in becoming acquainted with a group and to the counselor attempting to validate other information available about a pupil.

ADMINISTERING THE SOCIOMETRIC QUESTIONNAIRE

The validity of the results of the sociometric questionnaire are often greatly reduced because little attention is paid to the procedures for administering it. Very often the questionnaire is given to pupils before enough rapport has been established to motivate them to answer the questions with sincerity and before enough care has been taken to rule out the possibility of overlooking a pupil who is absent that day. Just as it is true with every form of data gathering technique, the information can be made more useful if the recommended practices for administering the instrument are carefully followed. The value of the responses to sociometric questions can be increased if the guidance worker will:

1. Be sure that every youngster knows how his responses will be used.

2. Use the technique only when the members of the class know each other well enough to make satisfactory choices.
3. Inform the pupils that their choices will be kept confidential.
4. Write the names of the pupils in the class on the board and point out any children who are absent.
5. Mention, especially to youngsters in the upper elementary grades, that it is all right to choose either boys or girls if this is so.
6. Allow a sufficient amount of time for each pupil to review the entire class before he writes down his choices.
7. Fulfill the agreement expressed or implied in the question as soon as possible.[11]

a final caution

Despite the many problems involved in organizing and administering an inventory service, it is easier to collect extensive information about students than it is to utilize it. In fact, the time spent in collecting various types of information may mount to such proportions that little is left for its use. Items or techniques should be added to the inventory program only after the need for them has been carefully considered and provisions have been made for utilizing the information collected. One step in this process is the organization of personal data into records which facilitate interpretation and use. It is appropriate, therefore, that the next unit be concerned with recording and interpreting information about students.

selected readings

Anastasi, Anne. *Psychological Testing.* Second Edition. New York: The Macmillan Company, 1961.

Buros, Oscar K. *The Fifth Mental Measurements Yearbook.* Highland Park, New Jersey: The Gryphon Press, 1959.

Durost, Walter N. and Prescott, George A. *Essentials of Measurement for Teachers.* New York: Harcourt, Brace, and World, Inc., 1962.

Froehlich, Clifford P. and Darley, John G. *Studying Students.* Chicago: Science Research Associates, Inc., 1952.

[11]Hatch and Costar, op. cit., pp. 68-69.

Froehlich, Clifford P. and Hoyt, Kenneth B. *Guidance Testing.* Chicago: Science Research Associates, Inc., 1959.

Goldman, Leo. *Using Tests in Counseling.* New York: Appleton-Century-Crofts, Inc., 1961.

Noll, Victor H. *Introduction to Educational Measurement.* Boston: Houghton-Mifflin Co., 1957.

Rothney, John W. M., Danielson, Paul J. and Heimann, Robert A. *Measurement for Guidance.* New York: Harper and Brothers, 1959.

Thorpe, Louis P., Whitson, Milo E., Baron, Denis, Adams, Georgia Sachs. *Studying Social Relationships in the Classroom: Sociometric Methods for the Teacher.* Chicago: Science Research Associates, Inc., 1959.

Traxler, Arthur E. *Techniques of Guidance.* Revised Edition. New York: Harper and Brothers, 1957.

White, Verna. *Studying the Individual Pupil.* New York: Harper and Brothers, 1958.

Warters, Jane. *Techniques of Counseling.* New York: McGraw-Hill Book Company, 1954.

Unit 3

The Pupil-Inventory Service

Recording and Interpreting Pupil Information

pupil information records

In the previous unit it was pointed out that information gathered by one technique of appraisal is subject to error or to misinterpretation and should therefore be checked against data available through other means. Similarly, evidence obtained during a given year frequently needs to be viewed in relation to the information gathered in both earlier and later years before its meaning becomes entirely clear. Frequently, also, the occasion for use of certain data comes at some time considerably after the collection period. When a student is in urgent need of assistance, it is not always practicable or possible to assemble at that moment all the information that would be useful. Each of these considerations suggests the need for a record system in which data are accumulated from year to year in some systematic and readily usable form.

TWO TYPES OF RECORDS

Two main types of records are used in schools, *administrative records* and *cumulative records.* Very often within these records there are various kinds of forms. Many of the forms deal with matters of only momentary importance, such as tardy and absence excuses, enrollment procedures, and the like. Other forms, such as rating scales or anecdotal record forms, may be of an intermediate nature; they provide a means of getting information for another and more permanent record system. In this unit we shall be concerned primarily with the permanent *cumulative record* system which is aimed at the guidance of individual students. Although they are essential, considerably less time will be spent discussing the customary, and usually separately maintained, record of courses, grades, and similar items which constitute the official *administrative record* of a student's passage through school. School responsibility and the necessity for security fully justify the existence of the latter type even though data in it often will be duplicated in the guidance record.

An administrative record form is shown in Figure 4. Such a record includes the information commonly required by law, including:

1. Name, age, birthdate
2. Date of entry into the school
3. Record of attendance
4. Record of achievement

Whether it is a legal requirement or a prerequisite for allocation of state funds, efficiency demands the maintenance of some such simple record requiring a minimum of clerical work and of storage space. Storage space is a particular problem because of the necessity for its being fireproof. Additional data desired for working with students usually can be placed in another more comprehensive *cumulative record.*

The nature of a *cumulative record* naturally depends upon the amount and kind of information to be kept. Generally speaking, it consists of all those items of information about the student which would be of assistance to teachers and counselors in helping him get the most out of his school experiences. As a minimum, it would include the items of essential information listed at the beginning of Unit Two. Cards of various sizes are commonly used to record such data and can be so organized as to include an astonishing amount of information, but they do not permit the filing of personal documents, letters, and other items not readily transferable to a form. A printed form folder can be used, but it is apt to become cumbersome as items accumulate in the folder. A combination record system involving a summarizing card and a folder for more bulky items has advantages but is relatively expensive to maintain. Some individuals prefer a folder which includes pockets for insertion of loose materials, thus making the process more syste-

NAME GRADUATED 19

YORK COMMUNITY HIGH SCHOOL

FIRST YEAR					SECOND YEAR					THIRD YEAR					FOURTH YEAR					FIFTH YEAR				
19	19				19	19				19	19				19	19				19	19			
SUBJECT	1ST	2ND	H P	CR	SUBJECT	1ST	2ND	H P	CR	SUBJECT	1ST	2ND	H P	CR	SUBJECT	1ST	2ND	H P	CR	SUBJECT	1ST	2ND	H P	CR
ENGLISH 9					ENGLISH 10					ENGLISH 11					ENGLISH 12									
ALGEBRA 9					GEOMETRY 10					MATH 11					MATH 12									
GEN BUS 9					COM L ARITH GEOG.					TYPING 11					STENOG 12									
GEN SCIENCE 9					BIOLOGY 10					PHYSICS 11					CHEM 12									
										SHTHD 11														
CLOTHING 9					FOODS 10															TOTAL HONOR POINTS				
																				TOTAL CREDITS				
FRENCH 9					FRENCH 10															KEY TO AND NOTES ON TRANSFERRED MARKS				
GERMAN 9					GERMAN 10					GERMAN 11														
SPANISH 9					SPANISH 10					SPANISH 11														
LATIN 9					LATIN 10					LATIN 11														
					HIST 10					HIST 11					HIST 12									
PHYS ED 2 HRS					PHYS ED 2 HRS					PHYS ED 1 HR					PHYS ED 1 HR					MAJORS				
TOTALS					TOTALS					TOTALS					TOTALS					MINORS				
DAYS ABSENT					DAYS ABSENT					DAYS ABSENT					DAYS ABSENT					WAIVERS				
TIMES TARDY					TIMES TARDY					TIMES TARDY					TIMES TARDY									

FINAL CREDITS | FINAL HONOR POINTS | RANK IN CLASS | NO IN CLASS | HONOR PT AV

LAST NAME | FIRST NAME | MIDDLE NAME | ADDRESS | PHONE

Part of record used in York Community High School, Elmhurst, Illinois. Reproduced through the courtesy of Remington Rand, Inc., 315 Fourth Avenue, New York 10, New York.

Figure 4

matic than just dropping them in an open folder. Figure 5 shows an end view of a folder of this type. The folder facings, both internal and external, can be printed with forms such as those illustrated in Figure 4. If desired, the pockets can be subdivided into smaller pockets. Special insert cards can be developed in appropriate sizes to fit these pockets. All insert cards should be designed at the same time so that they fit a common pattern and can be used together easily. Using a different colored card for health information, test data, and other distinct catagories is a valuable aid to locating recorded information in a folder of this type.

administrative problems in record keeping

In many schools today the concept of two different types of information is recognized, but in others both kinds of data are classified under the same broad title of pupil information. Many problems grow out of the broader interpretation. Some of the following problems are illustrative:[1]

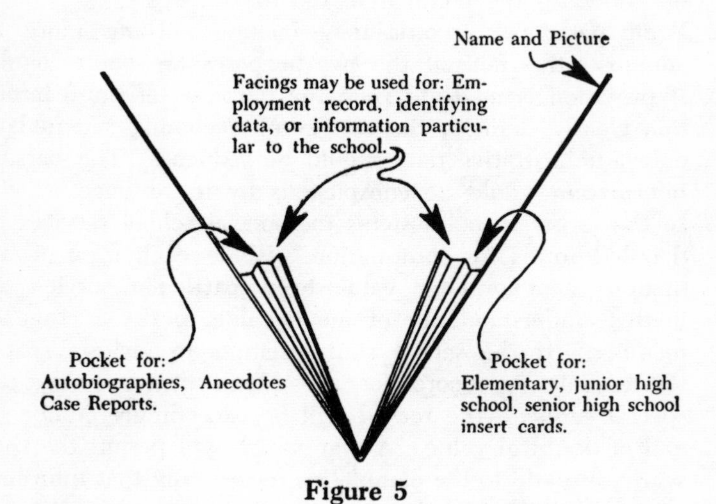

Figure 5

1. Much contention is to be found in the housing of the records. The administrative staff is responsible for the safekeeping of the administrative information and may insist on housing

[1]Raymond N. Hatch and James W. Costar. *Guidance Services in the Elementary School.* Dubuque, Iowa: Wm. C. Brown Company Publishers, 1961, pp. 87-88.

it in the fireproof vault in the central office. The guidance worker is aware of the need to have the personnel information near the individuals who will use it while working with boys and girls. Both objectives seem valid, but keeping the two kinds of information in the same record tends to prevent both the administrative and guidance staffs from fulfilling their obligations. Recognition of two kinds of information and the setting up of a record keeping system to handle it will reduce staff contention.

2. Keeping the two kinds of information in the same record increases the clerical work of the teaching staff. Recording the class marks and attendance records in the cumulative record each marking period adds more work to the teacher's duties but offers little to the content of the cumulative record that will be useful to the classroom teacher or counselor. Such information is necessary for administrative purposes, but a semester average or total is usually all that needs to be added to the cumulative records.
3. Pupil personnel records may include nothing more than administrative facts if the two purposes are not recognized. If provision is made to keep the purposes of pupil information clearly defined, the danger of becoming satisfied with only administrative data should be reduced. The personnel information would be conspicuous by its absence.
4. In the larger school systems the special school services have detailed forms for information. While each type of information is of primary value to a particular service, it is neither understood nor of much value to the average staff member. If the school staff attempts to include space in the cumulative record for the administrative forms of all special services, the record will be exceedingly cumbersome and of doubtful value. A plan which will permit the special services to add to the cumulative record only that information about a pupil which has a direct bearing on his adjustment would seem advisable.

the cumulative record

VALUES OF THE CUMULATIVE RECORD

The cumulative record system provides an opportunity to know and understand students as individuals. In most high schools today a student has several teachers and these may change from semester to semester. Each instructor likewise has many different students. The result is that most teachers know only a few facts about individual students; and unless some technique is employed to bring all the information together, it is likely that few will see any student as an integrated personality. Even those teachers who do attempt to see students as "whole" individuals will become discouraged by the difficult task of assembling the necessary information alone.

Cumulative records facilitate the study of long-term development of students. Changes in behavior over a period of several years, whether they be desirable or undesirable, are not likely to be detected by teachers who work with the student for only a few months. Moreover, movement toward the broader, long-term educational objectives of the school is apt to be slow unless such records are kept to help teachers and counselors chart the course of progress.

The cumulative record system can be the basis for encouraging self-appraisal and self-understanding by each student. Such steps are important in developing personal and social adjustment. Awareness of strengths and weaknesses and concrete evidence of improvement are perhaps the most potent means of encouraging further development in the normal child.

CHARACTERISTICS OF THE CUMULATIVE RECORD

The cumulative record should be developed with some very definite objectives in mind. The following characteristics are usually considered as the minimum essentials of a good cumulative record:

1. It should show chronological growth and development.
2. It should contain space for all information considered pertinent to a better understanding of the pupil.
3. It should be organized so as to provide for a continuous recording of data about the pupil from kindergarten through the secondary school.
4. Space should be provided for the inclusion of autobiographies, anecdotes, and other loose materials.
5. Major content should be organized so as to demand the least amount of time and effort for recording by providing categories where the appropriate data can simply be checked.
6. The form should provide space for tests and similar information peculiar to a given school within the system.[2]

[2]Ibid., p. 90.

Several commercial cumulative record folders are now available similar to the one published by Doubleday Brothers and Company.[3] It consists of a printed manila folder along with insert cards of different colors for elementary and junior high school scholastic and family data, high school scholastic and family data (see Figure 6), health information, and reading progress. Special provisions are made for recording the transfer of these records from school to school with the child. Most school systems find that it is necessary to make some modifications in commercially purchased forms in order to meet the unique needs of their schools. Many prefer to develop their own folders rather than make a sizable number of changes.

DEVELOPING A CUMULATIVE RECORD SYSTEM

One of the first steps in the development or revision of a cumulative record system should be that of analyzing the objectives of the school in determining what data are related to them. Our discussion of records assumes that there is a set of objectives understood and accepted by the teachers, counselors, and administrators. A content-centered teaching staff will have little interest in information beyond that related to achievement. The other types of evidence available in records will be ignored as irrelevant to their purposes except in the cases of students who are foci of disturbance in the classroom. Acceptance of broad objectives for behavior change brings a desire for records which will show for each student:

1. All significant and relevant past or needed social experiences related to the total development of the student.
2. Data needed to verify academic achievement or to facilitate it.

The implication of these two points is that a cumulative record system should not be thought of solely as a place to find out what has happened to the student but also as a source of information for planning what experiences he should have in the future. The difference lies in whether or not the record system itself is planned in terms of clearly defined objectives. If it is, it has a framework within which the information about a student can be systematically analyzed so that deficiencies in his academic and social develop-

---

[3] *Cumulative Record Folder,* Form No. CA-60, Kalamazoo, Michigan: Doubleday Brothers and Company, 1960.

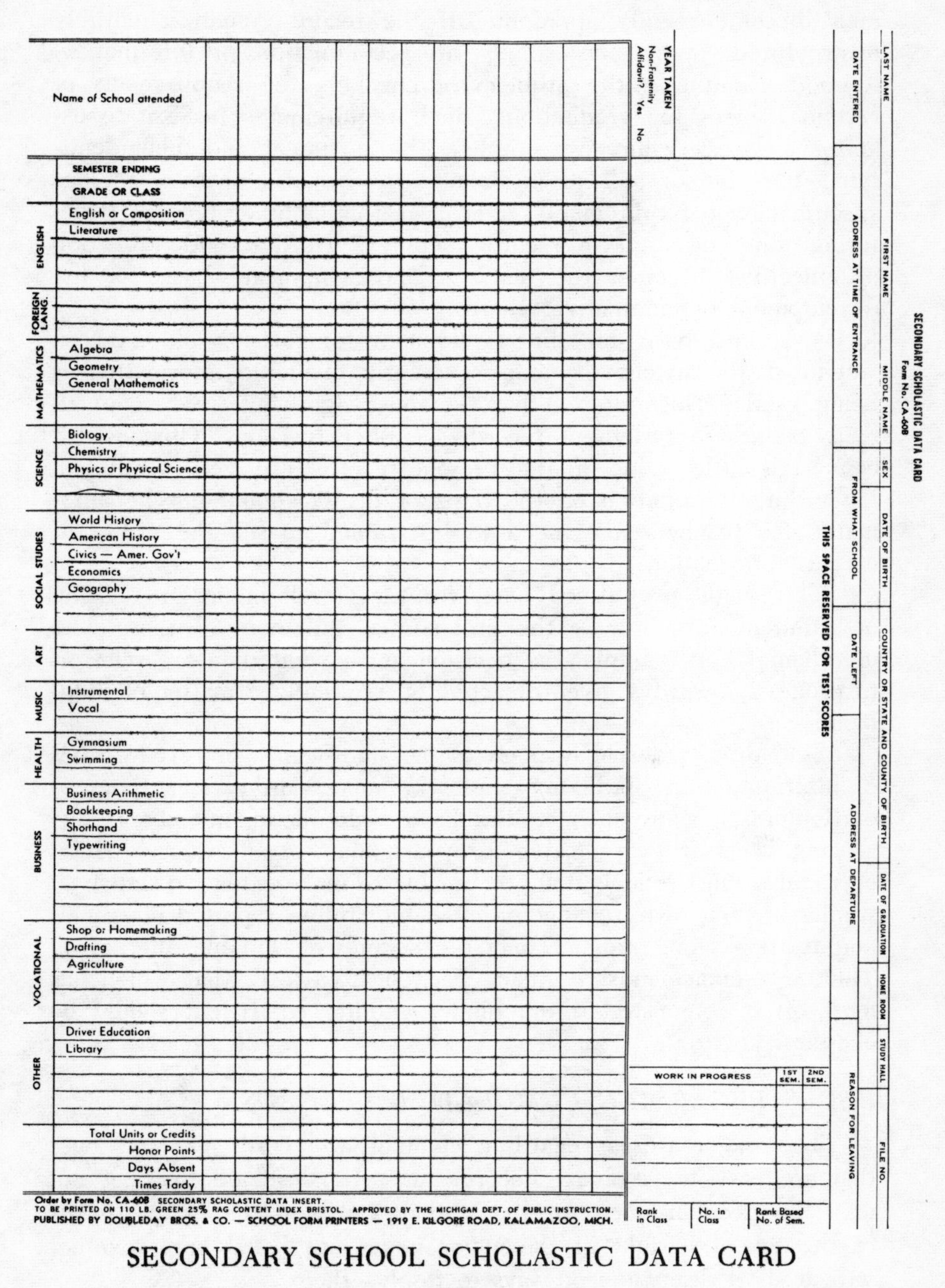

SECONDARY SCHOLASTIC DATA CARD
Form No. CA-60B

LAST NAME
FIRST NAME
MIDDLE NAME
SEX
DATE OF BIRTH
COUNTRY OR STATE AND COUNTY OF BIRTH
DATE OF GRADUATION
HOME ROOM
STUDY HALL
FILE NO.

DATE ENTERED
ADDRESS AT TIME OF ENTRANCE
FROM WHAT SCHOOL
DATE LEFT
ADDRESS AT DEPARTURE
REASON FOR LEAVING

THIS SPACE RESERVED FOR TEST SCORES

YEAR TAKEN
Non-Fraternity Affidavit? Yes No

Name of School attended

SEMESTER ENDING
GRADE OR CLASS

ENGLISH
English or Composition
Literature

FOREIGN LANG.

MATHEMATICS
Algebra
Geometry
General Mathematics

SCIENCE
Biology
Chemistry
Physics or Physical Science

SOCIAL STUDIES
World History
American History
Civics — Amer. Gov't
Economics
Geography

ART

MUSIC
Instrumental
Vocal

HEALTH
Gymnasium
Swimming

BUSINESS
Business Arithmetic
Bookkeeping
Shorthand
Typewriting

VOCATIONAL
Shop or Homemaking
Drafting
Agriculture

OTHER
Driver Education
Library

Total Units or Credits
Honor Points
Days Absent
Times Tardy

WORK IN PROGRESS	1ST SEM.	2ND SEM.

Rank in Class
No. in Class
Rank Based No. of Sem.

Order by Form No. CA-60B SECONDARY SCHOLASTIC DATA INSERT.
TO BE PRINTED ON 110 LB. GREEN 25% RAG CONTENT INDEX BRISTOL. APPROVED BY THE MICHIGAN DEPT. OF PUBLIC INSTRUCTION.
PUBLISHED BY DOUBLEDAY BROS. & CO. — SCHOOL FORM PRINTERS — 1919 E. KILGORE ROAD, KALAMAZOO, MICH.

SECONDARY SCHOOL SCHOLASTIC DATA CARD

Figure 6

ment become readily apparent. If the record system is entirely unstructured, it becomes simply an accumulation of information. A good example is the problem of checking the requirements of certain courses for graduation. Such requirements necessitate examining the work already completed by a student and then identifying the courses still to be taken. As broad objectives replace specific course requirements, it is clear that another type of structuring must be used in record keeping. Thus, the identification of objectives becomes the first and most important basis for the development of cumulative records.

A second basis for the development or revision of a record system is the extent to which presently available information is being used. This criterion has the most significance when an already extensive system of records is under revision. Obviously it can have little value if the present records are very restricted. Discarding information on the basis of disuse should not be automatic, for teachers may need to be trained to see the utility of certain information.

This leads to a third basis for the development or revision of cumulative records — the professional judgment of those who use them. For example, the decision as to what data are relevant to progress toward a given objective is frequently a matter of judgment.

Statistical studies may point to the significance of certain types of information in predicting grades or success in various types of curriculums. Many such studies have been made, but the results are not necessarily applicable to a particular school system. However, since most schools will not be able to make extensive statistical studies of their own, reliance on available studies reported in articles and textbooks on guidance may be the only reasonable alternative. Thus, if a choice must be made between two tests, that which has most often demonstrated the higher validity coefficient should be chosen.

ISSUES REGARDING CUMULATIVE RECORDS

The major isuses regarding cumulative records are not ones that are easy to resolve. Records must be designed to meet not only the peculiar needs of the student but also the unique needs of the school. Eight of the major issues are listed here together with a short discussion of ways to resolve them.

1. Uniformity vs. individuality

It may seem contradictory, but the record system which has its origin in concern about individual differences must achieve a degree of uniformity by providing the same general types of information on all students and a standard form for recording it. Failure to provide any uniformity makes the records so difficult to use that they will be of little practical value. This consideration effectively rules out a system based entirely on accumulating isolated bits of information in a folder and suggests the need for a printed form involving a planned organization of all items of information.

2. Objectivity vs. subjectivity

Many traits and behaviors of students can be reported only on a subjective basis, but objectivity represents a goal toward which everyone contributing to records should strive. The more subjective items which inevitably reflect the personality of the reporter should include the name of the reporter.

3. Accessibility vs. restrictivity

Records which are to be helpful to teachers in understanding students must be readily accessible to them. When teachers must first clear with a clerk, counselor, or principal there is less use made of the records. Likewise, each student, through a teacher or counselor, should have ready access to his own record but certainly not to that of other students. The implication of such accessibility is that certain highly confidential materials will *not* become a part of the permanent record system but will remain in the personal file of the person receiving the information. Accessibility also requires some weighing of possible misuse by an unwise teacher against the disuse resulting from restrictivity. While such misuse is to be avoided, controls which eliminate it will also greatly reduce the effectiveness of the record system. It is more appropriate over a long period of time to provide in-service training in the use of records for teachers who are not well informed in this area.

4. Continuity vs. irregularity

Records to which items are contributed only at specified times or at highly irregular intervals are unlikely to represent a sufficiently broad sample of behavior to be truly helpful in understanding a student. Such practices undermine the records' usefulness and will probably result in ultimate abandonment of the system because it is viewed as having little value.

5. Simplicity vs. complexity

Some middle position on this continuum must be the goal. Simplicity must be sought only insofar as it is consistent with the nature of the data collected. Hence, the achievement of simplicity becomes mainly a matter of careful organization of the records and of the reporting forms so as to minimize the clerical work and the process of interpretation. For example, preprinted items which can be checked rather than blanks requiring the writing of a complete answer are simpler for the student to fill out and, because of the standardization, are more easily understood by anyone referring to them. Such convenience must be weighed against the probable loss in individuality of responses.

6. Benevolence vs. malevolence

This issue involves an in-service training program with teachers. Many teachers are conscious primarily of undesirable behaviors and are, therefore, inclined to report only these. Subconsciously these teachers may view the record as a disciplinary device or as a way to relieve their own aggressions. Clearly, to emphasize the association of cumulative records with discipline will reduce their value for helping the nondisciplinary student.

7. Utility vs. curiosity

A frequent objection to record systems is that the request for and filing of information involve an invasion of privacy. This objection goes hand in hand with a natural concern about who uses records and for what purposes. Most humans do have considerable curiosity with respect to the private lives of others. Casual chatter about humorous or unusual items on the record is to be avoided. Each such comment encourages more like it, resulting in an ultimate letdown in ethics and student and parental rebellion against the system. The earlier cautions with regard to the legality and wisdom of including certain types of information in the file should be kept in mind.

8. Commission vs. omission

Records are likely to show more of what a student has done than of what he has failed to do. Thus, the student who makes a nuisance of himself by violent handwaving in a desire to recite may inspire the teacher to report. The student who never volunteers may be overlooked, and the absence of any item on the record would seem to imply normality in this respect. The absence of certain types of behavior is just as significant as the presence of others.

DIEDERICH PROFILE INDEX

One of the most difficult problems in cumulative records is the development of some simple technique for relating the information to school objectives. Several years ago Dr. Paul Diederich of the Educational Testing Service proposed a "Profile Index" which contains an individual profile for each student, listing the objectives of the school and providing a way of quickly relating the accumulated evidence to these objectives. The following brief description is extracted from a dittoed statement prepared by Diederich, and used here with his permission. The accompanying profile of objectives is probably more extensive than would be wanted by any one school, but it is obvious that the list of objectives on the profile could be constructed or revised to suit the need of any school.

> The appended "Profile Index" is designed to keep track of data on pupil development and to give at a glance some idea of what these data mean. It is NOT a rating scale. At no time does any teacher or counselor record on the Profile Index his subjective opinion of any aspect of a pupil's growth. It assumes that teachers in all fields will be collecting *evidence* at various times through the year on those aspects of pupil development which the school regards as important. As soon as these teachers are through with the evidence for their own purposes, instead of dumping it in a wastebasket, they deposit it in a box in the central office. A clerk will then sort it into the mailboxes of the counselors of the pupils concerned. The counselors are responsible for filing this material in the pupils' folders and for recording it at the same time on the Profile Index. They do so as follows.
>
> Let us assume that Counselor X finds two pieces of evidence in his mailbox. The first is a form labeled "Record of Incomplete and Unsatisfactory Work." It indicates that Mary Smith failed to complete an important assignment in English on the due date: the excuse she wrote on the form at the time

was unconvincing; she suggested a later date for completing the assignment but missed it by three days; and the teacher's comment on the affair was most unfavorable. If the school is systematic in its collection of data, this evidence will probably come in labeled "B12-W" indicating that it refers to the objective numbered B12 in the Profile Index ("get things done on time"), and that it shows a *weakness* in this aspect of development. After perusing this bit of evidence, the counselor opens Mary Smith's folder and finds that there are already 26 pieces of assorted evidence in it; that is, the piece on top is numbered 26. The new evidence, then, becomes number 27. The counselor writes this number on the top of the new evidence and places it in the folder. The counselor then writes the number 27 on Mary's Profile Index (which is always uppermost in her folder) opposite objective B12 and in the column labeled "Weak."

The second piece of evidence is a biology test taken by John Jones. The teacher's notations indicate that it refers to objective F1, knowledge of the natural sciences, and shows *strength* in this area; also to objective F13, interpreting data, in which the student placed in the middle half of the group tested – a status which the Profile Index calls "*average.*" Since there are already 34 pieces of evidence in Jones' folder, the new one becomes number 35. The counselor writes this number on the top of the test and places it in the folder on top of number 34. He then writes the number 35 in two places on John's Profile Index: opposite objective F1 in the column labeled "Strong," and opposite objective F13 in the column labeled "Average."

As the Profile Index fills up with numbers, it will show at a glance the aspects of development on which the school has collected data for any given pupil and the degree of attainment of each objective indicated by the evidence. If the counselor is worried by the weakness revealed in any area, such as "exercises self-control," he can instantly locate the evidence bearing on this objective, for the numbers written after it will tell him the serial order of this evidence in the folder. If the counselor does not have time to write down *one number* for each piece of evidence that he gets, it is plain that no record at all will be kept, for it is impossible to write less than one number.

The evidence will simply be dumped into folders without passing through the mind of anyone who knows the pupil. As the folders fill up with unassorted evidence, the task of reading it and making any sense at all of it will become impossible. Then the folders may as well be thrown away.

The appended Profile Index uses as its main headings six major values which are commonly held to be essential elements of a good life or of happiness under present conditions of life in our society. The objectives listed under these values are believed to increase the chances of attaining these values, both individually and collectively. More objectives are listed than any one school would want to use; rather, each school would use its own list and might easily get it on one or two pages. The columns labeled "Weak," "Average," and "Strong" refer usually to standing in the lowest quarter, the middle half, or the top quarter of the group tested — or, less precisely, to unfavorable, average, or favorable evidence. If a test yields an exact percentile rating on national or local norms, the number should be recorded as near this point as possible; each dot represents five percentile points. The crowding of dots in the center is intentional; normally the interquartile range on a test is shorter than either the top or bottom quarters. Some space is left at the bottom of each page for additional objectives to be written in as they are adopted.

It is hoped that schools will gradually abandon marks in courses as their sole record of the development of their pupils. Instead teachers should collect evidence of the development of those characteristics which increase the chances of attaining happiness, both as individuals and as a society. The collection of such evidence should not be left to chance — although, once the system is established, a great deal of valuable evidence will come in by chance. A standing committee on evaluation should decide what evidence is needed and where it can be gathered most conveniently. It should schedule the collection of specified evidence at times scattered throughout the year, so as not to overburden any pupil or teacher. It should see to it that the evidence flows in to counselors, clearly marked with the number of the objective or objectives to which it refers and with a letter or other symbol (e.g., a percentile rank) for the degree of attainment of each objective which it indicates.

It should make certain that the evidence passes through the mind of someone who knows the pupil and who feels responsible for his all-round development. The Profile Index will both stimulate and facilitate these processes. After some further development it ought to be adopted at least as a supplement to, and possibly as a substitute for, the present system of academic bookkeeping.

The Profile Index

A. LIFE-MAINTENANCE	WEAK 0	25	AVERAGE 50	75	STRONG 100
Necessities (food, clothing, etc.)					
1. Knows how our own and other economic systems operate					
2. Knows about distribution of chief natural resources; resists wasting them					
3. Respects property rights, contracts, and regulations affecting them					
Practical competence in					
4. shopping, buying wisely					
5. cooking, serving, dining					
6. cleaning, keeping things in order					
7. caring for children					
8. making things, making repairs					
9. care of house, grounds, property					
10. care of money, banking, insurance					
11. traveling, driving a car					
Health					
Healthful attitudes:					
12. Security: self-confidence, poise, independence, flexibility, cheerfulness					
13. Affection: is able to give and receive affection freely; shows good will toward others, etc.					
14. Health knowledge: physiology, psychology, hygiene, etc.					
15. Health habits: diet, play, rest, cleanliness, medical care, etc.					
16. Public health: supports and obeys public health measures					
17. Safety: obeys safety regulations, takes reasonable precautions					

B. SENSE OF WORTH OR ACHIEVEMENT	WEAK 0	25	AVERAGE 50	75	STRONG 100
1. Is developing a picture of self and of an acceptable role in life which can be sustained					
2. Sets reasonably high standards and tries to live up to them					

Figure 7

3. Has sense of belonging to a social group without undue dependence on it
4. Wins recognition and acceptance for desirable traits or accomplishments
5. Is developing vocational interests and competence
6. Regards occupation as a contribution to the common welfare, not as a struggle to take something away from others

Work habits or traits:

7. self-direction, initiative
8. industry, perseverence, thoroughness
9. honesty, responsibility
10. good judgment, decisiveness
11. orderliness, system, neatness
12. gets things done satisfactorily and on time

C. FRIENDLY RELATIONS WITH OTHERS — WEAK 0 — 25 — AVERAGE 50 — 75 — STRONG 100

1. Likes people
2. Takes reasonable care of appearance
3. Has a pleasant speaking voice
4. Can entertain others in conversation
5. Can dance, take part in group singing, and play popular games
6. Is courteous, tactful, pleasant
7. Is honest, candid, truthful
8. Is tolerant
9. Has a sense of humor
10. Exercises self-control
11. Is willing to help others
12. Can work and play with others without quarreling
13. Can assume leadership when necessary
14. Can assume a subordinate role when necessary
15. Has desirable atttiudes towards the opposite sex
16. Has desirable attitudes toward parenthood
17. Is willing to assume family responsibilities

D. A FREE SOCIETY — WEAK 0 — 25 — AVERAGE 50 — 75 — STRONG 100

1. Shows interest in and concern for the general welfare
2. Sees social significance of current happenings
3. Relates present issues to their historic background

Figure 7 (Continued)

4. Has consistent and enlightened attitudes toward current social issues
5. Can discover, evaluate and present facts relevant to social issues
6. Can detect propaganda
7. Knows techniques of social action (e.g., how to get a law passed)
8. Is willing to devote time, money, and effort to public affairs
9. Respects law and its agencies
10. Accepts majority decisions
11. Values, respects, and defends basic human rights (free speech, etc.)
12. Knows, accepts, and values the American heritage of self-government
13. Realizes that a good life can be attained only by organized cooperation
14. Is willing to defend country against aggression or tyranny
15. Knows about, critically evaluates, and supports all promising efforts to prevent war

E. AESTHETIC EXPERIENCE — WEAK (0, 25) — AVERAGE (50) — STRONG (75, 100)

1. Seeks contact with nature and finds refreshment in it
2. Practices at least one of the arts and enjoys several
3. Is moved emotionally and stirred intellectually by literature
4. Listens to good music on the radio and phonograph
5. Can sing a part in group singing or play a musical instrument
6. Responds to artistic qualities in painting and other visual arts
7. Appreciates dramatic qualities of the better motion pictures
8. Appreciates drama on the stage and on the radio
9. Appreciates architecture, interior decoration, city and regional planning
10. Appreciates design, color, and workmanship in objects of daily use
11. Brings order and beauty into the environment whenever it is possible

Figure 7 (Continued)

the uses of cumulative data

The educational philosophy of a school ultimately determines the use made of information in cumulative records. Records, no matter how complete or how available, are only a means to an end. The purposes or objectives of major concern in a school dictate the uses to which records will be put. As a consequence, overhasty expansion of records beyond the interests of a school faculty is to be avoided, because the expense is hardly justifiable and because the reaction against the expense and the extra effort involved may actually bring about a setback to the guidance program. This caution, however, should not lead one to ignore the fact that the existence of information about students and the gradual introduction of it into the daily thinking of the faculty is an effective way to arouse more and more interest in a broad program of guidance services. Records and associated pupil personnel activities should be ahead of faculty practice but not so far ahead as to incur faculty displeasure. Continual awareness of the various uses of records and an in-service training program to acquaint the faculty with these uses is perhaps the most constructive way of dealing with this educational problem.

The possible uses of records can be grouped under three major headings.

EDUCATIONAL

Educational uses include the following:

1. Enhancing student development, self-appraisal, self-guidance
2. Making educational and vocational plans
3. Writing reports to or holding conferences with parents
4. Writing recommendations to prospective employers or to colleges

These uses form a minimum list of uses which might be found in any school. The more extensive the records, the more value they have, but schools can and do carry out the four functions listed even with rather sketchy records.

THERAPEUTIC

As teachers develop a greater awareness of individual personalities or as a counseling service is established, the following uses of records become important:

1. Early detection and prevention of maladjustment
2. Assistance to students on personal-social problems
3. Case conferences
4. Referrals to specialized professional or clinical agencies

Such use of records requires extensive information and a much higher degree of sophistication and psychological insight than the purely educational uses.

ADMINISTRATIVE

The administrative use of cumulative records includes:

1. Identifying and providing for special talent
2. In-service education of teachers
3. Evaluation of the school instructional and pupil personnel program

In a sense, this use of records involves an attempt to study information about an entire group of students, either to identify subgroups deserving special attention or to arrive at certain conclusions which help determine the effectiveness of a program and to point out ways in which it can be improved.

The range of uses suggested here may not include all the specific ones which occur in practice, but they do indicate the various viewpoints from which records can be approached. In general, intensity and range in the use of records go hand in hand with expansion of the range and variety of information placed in the records. Some balance between time spent in building up records and time spent in using records is a necessity. In a well-organized records program, use and recording may actually merge as well as supplement each other, since acquiring and recording additional items of information related to already available information may provide the basis for initiating some contact with the student or those associated with him.

some principles of educational diagnosis[3]

Understanding and predicting human behavior are extremely complex processes. Teachers and guidance workers are constantly

---

[3]Much of the remainder of this unit has been adapted from Raymond N. Hatch and James W. Costar. *Guidance Services in the Elementary School.* Dubuque, Iowa: Wm. C. Brown Company Publishers, 1961.

formulating tentative hypotheses about pupils as a part of their regular day-to-day activities. This informal method of analyzing the behavior of pupils can be improved in most cases by more formalized and systematic procedures. Some basic principles governing the diagnosis of pupil behavior are:

1. The accuracy of any diagnosis is only as good as the validity of the items of information used to make it. Inaccurate data is more misleading than helpful.
2. The behavior of the student can be understood only when it is examined within his total environment. Most behavior has many causes and is influenced by pressures from many sources.
3. A single test score or a single item of information is of little value in explaining the behavior of the child. The guidance worker should be looking for a pattern of behavior.
4. The behavior of each student should be studied in relation to his own consistent behavior as well as with that which is typical of his peer group. Atypical behavior may provide the clues which explain the child's actions.
5. Understanding a child just for the sake of understanding is of no real value in the school setting. New insights gained by the teacher should be used to develop better self-understanding on the part of the student and to create the most desirable learning conditions for that child.
6. The secondary school pupil is a rapidly growing and changing human being. Therefore any recommendations for helping him must be continually reassessed and revised. Teachers should be careful not to "peg" a student.
7. In most cases, more valid insights will be developed at a faster rate if two or more guidance workers exchange ideas about a particular student. The case conference approach is becoming increasingly popular with many different agencies and groups working with individuals under a variety of circumstances.

INTERPRETING THE DATA

The underlying purpose behind the entire pupil-inventory service of the guidance program is to assist each pupil to understand himself and to be understood as an individual. Thus the information which is collected and recorded can be of little value unless it is interpreted for the benefit of the student. Interpretation may be by the teacher for his own information; it may be to the student or his parents; it may be to other staff members; or it may include all three approaches. Regardless of the scope of the interpretation, certain fundamental concepts should undergird the study of information about students. The following are a few of the most important:

1. Interpretation should be based on all verified information, not just a few more readily accessible or interesting facts.
2. Interpretation should start with the complimentary factors and move to the less complimentary factors.
3. Uncomplimentary factors should not be mentioned unless they have been substantiated by sufficient data.
4. Exact numbers are frequently misleading; ranges may be more desirable.
5. Pupil information serves as a basis for the discussion of future action.
6. The information never sets exact limits for an individual but offers clues as to the probable capabilities of the student.
7. Interpreting the cumulative record is hazardous unless it includes information in all of the significant areas of student information.
8. Interpretation is "student-centered" since the information is peculiar to one individual and must be interpreted as one record. This makes it virtually impossible to set down specific information to be obtained from all records. Suggestions as to the possible uses of data would seem appropriate.
9. When students and parents are involved, it is better to interpret the information *with* them rather than *to* them. Active participation on the part of the pupil or parent not only serves as a guide for the person conducting the interview but increases the effectiveness of this type of learning situation by placing the counselee in the role of an active participant.

DEVELOPING A CASE STUDY

Several techniques have been devised to assist in the analysis of accumulated data about human beings. Scattergrams and case conferences are mentioned in a later chapter as specific methods of analyzing pupil information in a school setting. The case study is another useful means of becoming better acquainted with students.

Occasionally the reader will hear a *case study* referred to as a *case history*. However, most guidance workers do not consider the two as being the same. A case history is most often described as a compilation of objective factual data about a child, his physical and psychological characteristics, his environment, and his life history. The case study includes, in addition to the case history, an analysis and interpretation of the significant data and the specific recommendations for working with the student. Most case studies are developed as written reports of the action taken in case conferences. Only on rare occasions is it worthwhile for one teacher or guidance worker to develop a case study alone. When it is an outgrowth of the case conference, the case study is one of the most comprehensive and effective techniques for studying individual pupils.

General outlines used as guides for developing case study reports are as varied as the purposes of the agencies and institutions in which the case study is being used. Each outline should be designed to meet the peculiar needs of the institution or group that is working with the child. When the case study is developed as a written report of the case conference, the guidelines will usually follow the broad steps taken in conducting the case conference. The following is a typical procedure for holding a case conference in a school setting.

Step one – *Statement of the Problem.* Case conferences are usually called because there is a recognizable need to study the behavior of a particular youngster. Clearly stating the problem at the beginning of the conference makes it possible for each of the participants to analyze the student information in terms of a specific situation.

Step two – *The Case History.* Prior to beginning the conference, the teacher or guidance specialist usually brings together all of the student information which will help the members of the case conference come to a more complete understanding of the child. During the initial stages of the meeting the participants are given an opportunity to make changes in the factual data of the case history section when it is found to be inadequate or inaccurate.

Step three – *Interpretations and Conclusions.* During this phase of the conference every effort is made to identify all the significant items of information in the case history and to draw valid conclusions from the data. In most cases several worthwhile conclusions will be drawn about a particular problem situation in which a child is involved.

Step four — *Recommended Action.* Identifying the problem and its probable causes is the major objective of the case conference. At this point it may be quite easy for the teacher to see what action he might take in helping the child overcome his difficulty. However, having the participants in the conference discuss the advisability of certain courses of action helps the teacher and guidance specialist obtain different ideas about approaches that can be taken and helps establish a more secure feeling in carrying out ideas that they have developed on their own. Writing the recommendations into the case study increases the likelihood that the child will be treated in a consistent manner over a longer period of time, because the information is then available to all staff members who are working with the youngster. A written report also makes it possible to evaluate the case conference at some future date.

THE CASE HISTORY

The case history section of the case study consists of factual information about the student reported without interpretations. The history must be written as clearly, concisely, and objectively as possible. The scope of the information reported varies from case to case. It depends upon the experience and maturity of the participants in the case conference and the type of problem that is being explored. Professionally mature guidance workers considering a relatively simply problem, can recognize the significance certain kinds of information have for them and, at the same time, see that other information is not likely to be closely assocated with the situation under consideration. For the inexperienced staff it is better to collect too much rather than too little data. The data in the case history usually falls in one of the following three major categories:

1. Home and Famiy Background (ages, father, mother, siblings, education of parents, occupations, personal characteristics, nationality, religion, condition of the home, family interests and customs.)
2. Physical and Emotional Health (present physical condition, childhood diseases, physical disabilities, emotional and social adjustment, choice of friends, unusual behavior, physical stature, attitudes, interests, ideals, and aspirations.)

3. School History (school grades, standardized test scores, school activities, courses taken, study habits, and special interests or talents.)

WRITING THE CASE STUDY

The style of writing used in the case study must be clear and concise in order to prevent misinterpretation. Objectivity is of the utmost importance. Case studies written in a "friendly letter" style tend to disguise the significant data by surrounding it with superfluous words that mislead the reader who is consequently unable to determine exactly what the writer is trying to say. It is especially helpful if clear distinctions are made between what is objective fact and someone's interpretation of the facts.

Even the form of the case study has a bearing upon its usefulness. The fact that the case study outline should be a functional one has already been discussed. Double spacing the typewritten report makes it easier to read and less cumbersome when the reader must continually refer back to certain sections of the report to refresh his memory. Underlining key words in each paragraph also makes it easier to locate significant data.

Since the case study is quite often a report of the findings of a case conference, it is extremely important that those insights and conclusions which have been developed are reported accurately. Case reports are often written in such a manner that it is difficult for anyone except the participants in the case conference meetings to feel certain that he knows exactly what the recorder intended to say. The following are some of the common errors that should be avoided when writing case studies.

1. A large portion of the report is based on subjective opinion rather than objective facts.
2. The form used makes it difficult to locate the pertinent information that is referred to repeatedly when the case is being discussed.
3. Valuable information used to draw certain conclusions in the conference is not reported in the case history.
4. The terminology that is used is too technical and difficult to understand.
5. Data gathered from secondary sources and never verified are incorrectly reported as objective facts.

6. Certain kinds of information may be omitted because the writer feels that it will be embarrassing to him or to subsequent readers.
7. A disproportionate amount of space is devoted to reporting colorful or shocking incidents.
8. The writer's own attitudes and beliefs are allowed to creep into the material.
9. Provisions are not made for reporting the student's perception of his problem and how it might be handled.

a word of caution

That the case study has considerable value for purposes other than diagnosis is a well-established fact. It is an excellent in-service training device. Inexperienced guidance workers can gain considerable knowledge about child growth and development, abnormalities in school children, remedial techniques, and referral sources available within the school and community by participating in case study discussions. The case study is also an excellent means of creating staff interest in initiating or expanding a program of guidance services. However, there is a major caution which the educator planning to use this technique should keep in mind. *It is a time-consuming technique!* Many man-hours are required to develop and carry out the recommendations of a good case study. Unless sufficient time is made available to interested staff members for such activities, too much effort may be spent in working with one child at the expense of all the others.

summary

In this unit considerable emphasis was placed upon the importance of systematic and objective recording and interpretation of information about students which will be of assistance to the guidance worker in helping each child attain the maximum of his potential. Much more could be written than appears here regarding the use of such information, but few teachers and counselors have difficulty discovering uses for the data once it has been collected and reported to them. The major concern of every school administrator is that personal data about students, in the hands of the naive staff member, may be used for more harm than good. Restricting the accessibility of the data restricts the use that can be made of it. A more reasonable approach would be to provide within the system sufficient in-service training in the collection, interpretation, and use of student information to assure each child that his school experiences will be as meaningful and worthwhile to him as possible.

selected readings

Adams, James F. *Problems in Counseling —A Case Study Approach.* New York: The MacMillan Company, 1962.

Brueckner, Leo J. and Bond, Guy L. *Diagnosis and Treatment of Learning Difficulties.* New York: Appleton-Century-Crofts, Inc., 1955.

Cottle, William C. and Downie, N. M. *Procedures and Preparation for Counseling.* Englewood Cliffs, N. J.: Prentice-Hall, Inc., 1960.

DeHaan, Robert F. and Kough, Jack. *Identifying Students with Special Needs.* Secondary School Edition. Chicago: Science Research Associates, Inc., 1956.

Dreikurs, Rudolf. *Psychology in the Classroom.* New York: Harper and Brothers, 1957.

Dunsmoor, Clarence C. and Miller, Leonard M. *Principles and Methods of Guidance for Teachers.* Scranton, Pennsylvania: International Textbook Co., 1949.

Handbook of Cumulative Records. A Report of the National Committee on Cumulative Records. Washington, D. C.: Superintendent of Documents, U. S. Government Printing Office, Bulletin, No. 5, 1944.

Helping Teachers Understand Children. Division of Child Development and Teacher Personnel. Washington, D. C.: American Council on Education, 1945.

Kough, Jack and DeHann, Robert F. *Helping Students With Special Needs.* Secondary School Edition. Chicago: Science Research Associates, Inc., 1957.

Marzolf, Stanley S. *Psychological Diagnosis and Counseling in Schools.* New York: Henry Holt and Company, 1956.

Traxler, Arthur E. *How to Use Cumulative Records.* Chicago: Science Research Associates, 1947.

Traxler, Arthur E. *Techniques of Guidance.* Revised Edition. New York: Harper and Brothers, 1957.

Unit **4**

The Information Service

The guidance program can help a student benefit to the maximum from his school experiences through the utilization of two general approaches. Pupil personnel services must help the student gain an understanding and acceptance of himself as the first objective. The second objective is to help him interpret his environment, past and present, and its effect upon him. It is in developing an understanding of the characteristics and demands of the environment that the student utilizes the information service. The requirements, restrictions, opportunities, and impingements of the student's social and physical environment constitute the general framework of information included in the information service.

There has been a tendency on the part of guidance workers in the past to neglect the information phase of the guidance program. This may be the result of many influences, but it cannot be attributed to a lack of appreciation by the students for the service. Unrealistic vocational goals, meager knowledge about training opportunities, little understanding of how to get along with others, and dozens of other weaknesses that seem to be characteristic of today's youth are reported in research studies made during the past three decades. The feebleness of this service may be the result of the guidance staff's being overwhelmed with the vastness of the job to be done. The authors are inclined to believe that the inadequacy of the information service has many causes of which the most important is the fact that the guidance worker often does not have a clear concept of the scope of the service or ways of implementing it.

three main areas of information

The information service has grown from the narrow concept of occupational information to the broader concept of occupational, educational, and personal-social information. In the process of evolution, the role of occupational information has not become less important; but the areas of educational and personal-social information have been lifted from the position of "poor cousins" and now have a role of equal respectability. It must be pointed out, however, that all three phases of the service are interrelated. Frequently, information of significance in all three areas will be found in the same source. The counselor need not be concerned about this condition when he is making every effort to provide the student with a balance of information from all three phases.

OCCUPATIONAL

The oldest and most extensive phase of the information service is that of occupational information. It pertains to up-to-date information about the status and entrance requirements of present occupations and the techniques for predicting trends in the various job fields. It includes methods of collecting, evaluating, and presenting the information in the most effective manner. In its broadest application, it permits the student to explore, analyze, and try out various occupations in his quest for a satisfactory vocational choice.

EDUCATIONAL

All information directly related to training opportunities can be thought of as educational information. The information given the entering seventh grader about the new junior high school, the curriculum of the senior high school, college scholarships and loans available, and information about training opportunities for the secondary-school graduate or dropout make up the major part of the educational information phase.

PERSONAL-SOCIAL

The third area of the information service, personal-social information, is quite broad and is just now gaining impetus in the guidance program. Much of the information has been scattered throughout the educational program in such a way that it has tended to leave major gaps in the information service. Personal-social information includes that information about individuals which will help the student understand himself better and show him how he can improve the effectiveness of his relationships with others. Since the individual has an ever-changing need for social information as he matures, it is of major importance that this phase be carefully coordinated in order to prevent duplication and to fill, with speed and efficiency, those gaps that occur.

sources of information

The data to be used in the information service are from two general sources. One important source of information is that obtained by local research, observation,and compilation. Another rich and very satisfactory source of information is that material which has been prepared by national authorities and is of interest to a large number of students. The first source is quite technical in nature and the research requires careful planning before the information which is collected will be valid. The prepared materials are much easier for school personnel to obtain and to utilize than are the materials from local research. Because of the particular nature of this book, it seems advisable to mention the research source quite briefly and to devote the major discussion to the prepared sources.

INFORMATION FROM LOCAL RESEARCH

The three primary methods of collecting information at the local level are the community occupational survey, the job analysis, and the follow-up study. The *community occupational survey,* as the name implies, is a survey of the local community of the workers as well as their jobs. It attempts to ascertain the occupational distribution of the community's population, to collect specific information about particular occupations, and to check for local occupational trends which may be developing. The exact emphasis to be placed on the local survey will depend on the purpose for which the study is made as well as the amount of time, personnel, and facilities available. However, a major concern of the secondary school guidance worker is the number and type of entry occupations in the local community which draw on high school age youth.

The collection of occupational information by the method of *job analysis* has become quite common in industrial, governmental, and private agencies in the past twenty years. The data collected are used as a basis for incentive plans, labor contract negotiations, employee selection, and as a means of improving the techniques of total operation. The basic data are presented in a form known as a job description. This information is frequently pooled with other data to give the student factual statements of the duties, requirements, and other factors of an occupation in a number of agencies. A more general description of the total field is called the occupational description.

The *follow-up study* is not concerned primarily with the collection of information which can be used directly by the student. It is worth noting, however, that information related to the total welfare of the student is obtained by this method. The guidance staff should always be alert for the informational possibilities in the data of the follow-up study. A more complete discussion of this method is to be found in Unit Six of this book.

INFORMATION FROM PREPARED SOURCES

The scope of prepared information available is so broad that the counselor or teacher will find problems in selecting, filing, and coordinating the material. The many occupational briefs, monographs, and books; the hundreds of audio-visual aids; the catalogues and dictionaries; and the occupational materials listed in other categories will make selection of utmost importance in this phase of the information service. As a general rule, it is desirable to ascertain the need for certain kinds of information before making a selection. Once the type of information needed has been determined, the guidance staff can choose more wisely from the descriptive brochures of the various publishers. Whenever possible, it is desirable to obtain one title in a series for examination before ordering several from the same sequence.

PRINTED INFORMATION MATERIALS

The most complete type of prepared information is to be found in publications classified as: brief, abstract, guide, monograph, description, or brochure. As a general rule, the term is prefaced with the appropriate adjective which describes the major emphasis of the bulletin; for example, "occupational brief" is one of the most common titles. Frequently, the terms have been used interchangeably. This has resulted in considerable confusion to the prospective user of the material.

It seems desirable to devote some space to a clarification of terms used to describe printed publications. The terms brief, abstract, guide, monograph, and description are usually in the title of occupational information. The terms brochure, booklet, book, or catalogue are most often used to describe educational and personal-social information. Two significant differences are to be noted among the terms used to describe occupational information. The *description* is either a *job* or *occupational description* and does not include present salaries or predictions of future trends. The other terms are used to describe very similar occupational information, and the primary difference in one of length. Of these the most common term is *brief* which is usually a four to six-page description of an occupation. The next most common term is *monograph* which may have as many as seventy or eighty pages of information and sells at a higher price. However, the authors of the various publications have not always followed this plan in selecting a title for their publications, and this makes it necessary to investigate the titles to be purchased before fair comparisons of publications are possible.

The contents of most publications devoted to occupational information follow a similar format. The following topics are typical of the major headings of the *brief* and *monograph*:

1. Duties in the Occupation
2. Desirable Personal Qualifications
3. Outlook and Opportunities
4. Requirements for Entrance
5. Probable Earnings
6. Sources of Additional Information

A note of warning to the guidance staff about the selection of this material seems appropriate. Since so many different publishers prepare the material with different purposes in mind, the quality of publications will vary to a marked degree. Selecting material which has been prepared by a reputable guidance agency or by a recognized guidance authority would be a desirable safeguard. Good information can be obtained from sources which are hard to evaluate; but the guidance staff must exercise extreme caution in the use of such data, or the information service may become one of misinformation.

EVALUATION OF PRINTED INFORMATION MATERIALS

Over a period of time the guidance staff in any school can become quite adept at evaluating printed information materials for use in their system. Occasionally, all that is needed to reach a decision to accept or reject the material is a few minutes to check such criteria as: authorship, date of publication, attractiveness and readability for the age level at which it will be used, sources of data included, and freedom from bias and subjectivity. When a more comprehensive evaluation is required, a detailed check list is helpful. Such check lists can be devised by the guidance staff to include all those features thought to be important in their program. Many prefer to use guides developed by their professional associations such as the one prepared by the Occupational Research Division of the National Vocational Guidance Association for checking the contents of an occupational monograph.

CONTENTS[1]

I. History of the occupation
II. Importance of the occupation and its relation to society
III. Duties
  A. Definition of occupation
    1. As determined by an official organization such as a union, trade, or professional association
    2. As given in the law, for example, licensing legislation for barbers, undertakers, and architects
    3. Carefully formulated definition acceptable to those in the occupation.
    4. As defined in the *Dictionary of Occupational Titles,* Revised Edition, United States Employment Service, Superintendent of Documents, Washington, 25, D. C., 1949.
      a. Specific job definitions can be found in Volume I of the *Dictionary of Occupational Titles.* These job definitions may not necessarily reflect the scope of the subject occupation. Volume II or Part IV of the *Dictionary, however,* will aid in determining the specific jobs embraced by the occupation. In such cases, job definitions from Volume I will serve as source data for the preparation of a composite definition for such occupation.
  B. Nature of the work
    1. Divisions of the work
    2. Specific tasks performed by workers
    3. Other occupations with which this work can be combined
    4. Tools, machines, and materials used in the performance of the work
IV. Number of workers enaged in occupation, (Give source, date, and area covered by the figures used)
  A. Present number
    1. Total number engaged in occupation
    2. Total males, under 18; over 18
    3. Total females under 18; over 18

[1]Occupational Research Division, National Vocational Guidance Association, "Standards for Use in Preparing and Evaluating Occupational Literature," *Occupations, The Vocational Guidance Journal,* XXVIII (Feb., 1950), pp. 320-22.

B. Distribution
  1. Geographical distribution: numbers in specific areas, states, and regions
  2. Number of workers from special population segments, as broken down in the United States Census

C. Trends and outlook
  1. Increase or decrease in number of workers
  2. Increase or decrease in number of workers in relation to population and other occupations
  3. Oversupply or undersupply of workers
     a. Reasons
     b. Centers of this maldistribution
  4. Trends affecting large numbers of workers
     a. Short-term fluctuations
     b. Long-term trends
     c. Annual number needed to replace those dropping out

V. Qualifications

A. Age
  1. Age range, if any, required for entrance
  2. Age range, if any, required for retirement
  3. Age qualifications preferred by employers

B. Sex

C. Special physical, mental, social, and personal qualifications, excluding those obviously necessary for success in all types of work

D. Special skills essential to performance on the job

E. Special tools or equipment essential for the performance of the job, which must be supplied by the worker

F. Scores on tests for employment or selection

G. Legislation affecting occupation
  1. Laws regulating occupation
  2. Requirements for license or certificate

VI. Preparation

A. General education
  1. Necessary for successful performance of duties
  2. Desirable for successful performance of duties
     a. Amount
     b. Special courses of value

B. Special training, including probable cost of training
  1. Necessary. The minimum special training for successful performance of duties
  2. Desirable
  3. Special courses of value
  4. Additional training recommended for advancement
  5. Training centers
     a. Schools offering special training for this occupation. List of accredited, approved, or recommended schools with names of accrediting agencies, if any
     b. Training on the job, such as apprenticeship system, classes in plant, in-service training for veterans, etc.
     c. Other types of training

C. Experience
  1. Minimum necessary to enter occupation
  2. Related experience in other occupations
  3. Experience desirable for entrance
     a. Type
     b. Amount

VII. Methods of entering
- A. Public employment service
- B. Special employment agencies
- C. Civil service examination
- D. Apprenticeship
- E. License, certificate, ect.
- F. Other methods and channels

VIII. Time required to attain skill
- A. Special apprenticeship or union regulations
- B. Length of period of instruction on the job
- C. Length of time before median and maximum rates of pay are reached

IX. Advancement
- A. Lines of promotion: jobs from which and to which workers can be promoted
- B. Opprtunity for advancement
  1. Difficulties or certainties of promotion
  2. Factors determining promotion
  3. Evidence, if any, of ratio between those in higher jobs and jobs described.

X. Related occupations
- A. Occupations to which jobs can lead
- B. Occupations from which one can transfer

XI. Earnings
- A. Beginning wage range
- B. Wage range in which largest number of workers is found
- C. Maximum wage received by most highly skilled
- D. Medin and average salary, if available, and differences for sex and age groups
  1. Deductions
     - a. Uniforms
     - b. Equipment
     - c. Other
  2. Supplements
     - a. Uniforms
     - b. Lunches or other meals
     - c. Commissions
     - d. Tips
     - e. Bonus
     - f. Overtime
     - g. Other
- E. Annual versus life earnings
- F. Regulations
  1. National legislation
  2. Minimum wage laws
  3. Labor Board rulings
  4. Union regulations
- G. Benefits
  1. Pensions
  2. Federal Old Age Security
  3. State unemployment insurance
  4. Other
- H. Rewards and satisfactions other than monetary

XII. Conditions of Work
- A. Hours
  1. Daily
  2. Weekly
  3. Overtime; frequency
  4. Irrgeular hours of shifts

5. Vacation, with or without pay
6. Regulations
   a. State and federal legislation
   b. Labor Board Rulings
   c. Union regulations

B. Regularity of employment
1. Reason for regularity or irregularity
2. If irregular
   a. Normal periods
   b. Busy periods
   c. Dull periods
   d. Frequency of shutdowns of plant
   e. Cyclical unemployment
3. Amount of irregularity
   a. Number of workers employed during various seasons
   b. Per cent of the force retained during lull periods
   c. Per cent of the force added as extra workers during busy periods
4. Attempts to regularize employment
5. Effect of seasonal employment on the worker
6. Effect of cyclical employment

C. Health and accident hazards
1. Special risks connected with the occupation and means of prevention
2. State legislation, such as compensation for occupational diseases
3. Mental health hazards

XIII. Organization

A. Employees
1. Function, purpose, activities, and strength. When there are two or more unions, technical or professional organizations for workers, the size of membership of each and other evidence of relative strength should be given if possible.

B. Employers
1. Function, purpose, activities, and size

XIV. Typical places of employment. An electrician, for example, may find employment in an electrical repair shop, powerhouse, maintenance department of factories using electrical machinery, with construction companies, or with a gas and electric company.

XV. Advantages and disadvantages not otherwise enumerated

XVI. Supplementary information

A. Suggested readings; books, pamphlets, and articles
B. Trade and professional journals
C. Motion pictures, filmslides, and other visual aids
D. Other sources of information, such as state and federal government departments, reports of United States census, state employment servic, Bureau of Labor Statistics, etc.
E. List of associations, firms, or individuals who can provide further information

PUBLISHERS OF PRINTED MATERIALS

Printed materials to be used in the information service are available from many sources. Commercial publishers, educational institutions, professional organizations, and business firms interested in public service have published a vast amount of occupational, educational, and personal-social information. New material is made available to the guidance worker at frequent intervals, but much of the old material soon goes out of print. Another factor to keep in mind is that the price may change considerably on very short notice. Some of the leading guides to printed information in all three areas are listed following; and it is suggested that a good place for the guidance worker to start is by turning to these and similar guides for the names and addresses of current publishers.

1. *Bibliography of Current Occupational Literature.* Guidance Information Review Committee. Washington, D. C.: National Vocational Guidance Association, 1959.
2. *Educators Guide to Free Guidance Materials.* Randolph, Wisconsin: Educators Progress Service, 1962.
3. *Guide to Occupational Materials in Career Planning.* Los-Angeles: County Superintendent of Schools Office, 1959.
4. *Occupational Information.* Max F. Baer and Edward C. Roeber. Second Edition. Chicago: Science Research Associates, Inc., 1958.
5. *Occupational Literature: An Annotated Bibliography.* Gertrude Forrester. New York: H. W. Wilson Company, 1958.
6. *Occupational Outlook Handbook.* Bulletin 1300, Bureau of Labor Statistics. Washington: Superintendent of Documents, 1961.
7. *The Information Service in Guidance: Occupational, Educational, Social.* Willa Norris, Franklin R. Zeran and Raymond N. Hatch. Chicago: Rand McNally and Company, 1960.

FILING PRINTED MATERIALS

The vast quantity of information available may encourage the guidance worker to collect a large volume of material without making adequate provisions for suitable storage of the information. Bound publications soon become a forest of confusion unless a filing plan is developed prior to their collection. Very often the school librarian assumes the responsibility for cataloging these volumes.

The guidance staff may wish to develop its own plan for filing unbound material, or obtain one of several different plans available from commercial publishers. Whether the plan is purchased or "homemade," it will probably follow either one or some combination of the two general methods of filing information. The most common method is to file the material in alphabetical order. The second most common method is a system based on the *Dictionary of Occu-*

pational Titles.[2] If the latter method is used, it involves more detailed coding which requires more supervision for proper maintenance than the alphabetical system. The decision as to the method for filing this information must be made by the local staff, but to have a plan which will encourage a maximum amount of use is of the utmost importance in insuring the success of the information service.

audio-visual materials

One of the richest untapped sources of information for the school's guidance program is the area of audio-visual aids. In recent years new publishers have produced a large number of different materials, and the publishers of long standing have added to their titles. The guidance worker should become acquainted with the vast amount of this kind of information available which will fulfill a real need in the information service.

Three major types of audio-visual aids are prepared for use in the information service. The most common is the *motion picture,* followed by the *filmstrip* and *chart* both having about the same significance for use in the guidance program. *Recordings* are also made for the purpose of giving information, but they have not enjoyed the popularity of the other three.

SOURCES OF AUDIO-VISUAL MATERIALS

Because of the expense involved in making them, audio-visual materials are often outdated, and the guidance worker should be cautioned to review all types of films carefully before presenting them to an audience. Evaluating these media is as important as it is to develop a critique for each piece of printed material.

Again, the publishers are too numerous to mention here. However, during the past year several excellent guides to guidance films and filmstrips in all three areas of the information service have appeared which make it relatively easy for the teacher or counselor to select audio-visual materials suitable for the high school student.

---

[2]*Dictionary of Occupational Titles.* United States Employment Service. Superintendent of Documents. Washington, D. C., 1949. (This is the standard reference for classification of occupations. There are three different volumes now active Vol. 1 – Definitions; Vol. II – Codes and Titles; Vol. IV. – Entry Occupations.)

1. *Films and Filmstrips for Career Guidance.* Office of Santa Clara County Superintendent of Schools in Cooperation with the State Department of Education, Sacramento, California, 1961.
2. *Films for Junior and Senior High School Guidance.* Bloomington, Indiana: Audio-Visual Center, Indiana University, 1961.
3. *Guidance.* Chicago: Coronet Films, Sales Department, Coronet Building, 1962.
4. *The Use of Films in the Guidance Program.* East Lansing, Michigan: College of Education, Michigan State University, 1961.

presenting information

The most complete collection of the best information available is of little value to the information service unless careful plans are made for presenting such material to the students. The exact manner of presentation should vary somewhat with each situation, but a few general observations can be made which apply to most information programs. The following principles should be basic considerations in conducting the information service.

1. The secondary school student needs a vast amount of information which can be used for exploration. The student is able to choose much more intelligently if he has had a broad exposure to a variety of informational materials.
2. The vast amount of information to be presented suggests a need for careful coordination in order to prevent duplication and gapping omissions.
3. Since the emphasis of the information service is on exploration, the information to be presented is usually of common interest to a group of students. Because it is significant for a group of students, most of the information should be presented as a group activity.
4. Occupational, educational, and personal-social information can be interpreted as an integral part of the academic program. If information is presented through regular course offerings, it adds interest and realism to the course and provides the classroom teacher with an ideal opportunity to contribute directly to the guidance program.

5. Because students need vast quantities of information, the secondary school information service must utilize every opportunity to present information. One or two specific activities are but a beginning to a complete program. The maturation of the student and the constant change in his environment support the contention that every staff person must be cognizant of the need to supplement and support the information service.

METHODS OF PRESENTING INFORMATION

The most effective information service is organized in such a way that the individual student has access to the material at all times. Many students will do the necessary reading and research on an occupation or social problem only when their interest is high. Even a short delay in obtaining the information needed to satisfy his curiosity often results in a loss of interest which may not return until he has passed the stage where such information will be of maximum assistance to him. The most efficient practice combines the individual approach with that of presenting information with wide appeal to students in groups.

In a book such as this, space does not permit an exhaustive review of the various methods by which the staff can present information materials. Mention of the more common methods is made here with the hope that the reader will find the references at the end of this unit helpful in making a more intensive study of those activities which appear promising to him.

Information File. The file of unbound information should be available for either casual or assigned reading by all students. The vertical drawer file is a suitable means of housing such material for library and classroom use. Most guidance staffs will find it helpful to have one file of information for full-time use in the library and another mounted on casters for classroom use. The latter file can be used by many different staff members as needed in their classroom activities.

Assembly Programs. The school staff is frequently seeking educational activities for the assembly programs. Student participation in skits, discussions, and as narrators for a filmstrip are but a few of the ways in which information can be presented in the assembly. Both motion pictures and outside lectures are excellent means of introducing information to the student body during the assembly meeting.

TEACHERS OFTEN PREFER TO TAKE THE OCCUPATIONAL INFORMATION FILE TO THEIR CLASSROOMS FOR A SHORT PERIOD OF TIME.

Care must be exercised in selecting material according to the age range of the audience, for the information can be either too mature or immature for the students in attendance. As a general rule, not more than four class levels should be in the assembly room for any information meeting. A group consisting of only two levels is even more desirable.

Clubs. Club activities are very common in the secondary schools of America. The clubs often devote considerable time to the interpretation of pertinent information related to the group's primary interest. For example, the physics club reviews the job outlook and training necessary for a career in physics; the future teachers' club follows a similar plan; while the dancing club uses this activity as a vehicle for interpreting social information. The role of student clubs in presenting information is an important one, and this particular function should be given special consideration by guidance specialists and faculty advisors.

Bulletin Boards. Alert and effective use of the bulletin board by guidance workers is an excellent means of placing a considerable amount of information before students. Two suggestions seem appropriate in the use of the bulletin board for presenting information. Material should never be posted unless it is somehow brought to the attention of the students, and information should be changed at frequent intervals. Careful use of the bulletin board can add much to the information program at all grade levels.

Special Days. Career and college days have long been a part of the information program at the secondary school level. It is not uncommon to find that the career day is the only identifiable information activity in the school. Although such a situation is unfortunate, there is an important place in the information service for the career and college day.

Special days often are used as a means of presenting exploratory information. Few activities could be more unrealistic than utilizing a one-day meeting as a method of exploring vocations or colleges. It is unrealistic because the student cannot hear about more than three or four different possibilities, and the information is usually presented by individuals who are quite biased in their presentation. The fact that the information is presented away from the true setting of the college or occupation adds to the unreality of exploratory information. What, then, is the role of the special day?

Many of the students in the eleventh and twelfth grades limit their occupational and educational choices to a few if given a good base of exploratory information. When the choices have been narrowed, the guidance staff can invite individuals representing the colleges and occupations of the students' tentative choices to act as referral people for answering specific questions. If the day is used as a referral day and not as an exploratory information day, it will be more satisfactory to the outside speakers and prove more effective in providing the student with meaningful information.

Orientation Programs. Orientation is a term which has been defined in the guidance literature in two ways. The more common use of the term refers to it as a single activity or a series of closely related activities. The less common usage of the word orientation is to refer to it as a continuous process. Both applications are acceptable, but the latter usage is much broader and tends to include activities of several other guidance services. The usage is based upon the definition of orientation as the ability to locate oneself in one's environment with reference to time, place, and people. As the student does this, he is assisted in the process by at least three guidance services: pupil-inventory, information, and counseling. Thus the use of the term orientation as a broad process causes some confusion and will not be used as such in this discussion.

Only those activities devoted to assisting the student gain an objective understanding of a new environment and a feeling of belonging in these new surroundings are considered here as part of the orientation program. Information about a new school setting, the physical layout, the staff, the students, the curricular and co-curricular offerings, and the regulations by which the school operates are typical kinds of information in the orientation program. Presenting information of this type usually requires many different approaches and may involve several different individuals or groups of individuals.

Many areas of information are discussed in orientation programs. The Division of Guidance and Child Accounting of the Pittsburgh Schools, under the direction of O. J. Schwarm, outlined an excellent group of items for orientation to senior high school. The following is taken from the publication of that office entitled, "A Plan For Group Guidance."[3]

1. The school plant
   a. Floor plan of the building
   b. The athletic field
2. School practices
   a. Daily schedule of classes
   b. Absence and tardiness regulations
   c. Early dismissal policies

[3]Reproduced through the courtesy of O. J. Schwarm.

d. Fire drill
e. Cafeteria procedures
f. Halls and lockers
g. Street car passes
h. Pupil's records
(1) Report cards
(2) Medical reports
(3) Cumulative records
(4) Permanent record cards
i. Lost and found
j. The library
k. Bookroom

3. School organizations
a. Homerooms
(1) Purpose and value
(2) Officers and committees
(3) Parliamentary procedure
b. Class groups

The techniques of presenting orientation information fall into several familiar categories. Student handbooks, big brother-big sister activities, visits to the new school, and various social groupings are the methods most often used in orientating students to the secondary school. All of these permit considerable latitude for the ingenuity of the guidance worker. Every opportunity should be provided for students and student groups to conduct their own orientation activities. The normal willingness of adolescents to participate wholeheartedly in activities of this type tends to increase the effectiveness of the orientation program.

The student handbook is an excellent project for the student council or other student organizations of the secondary school. The students can present the information in a manner which has appeal to other students and they themselves will profit from the experience. The handbook can be prepared in either printed or illustrated form. Many high schools have developed the cartoon idea, which has proved very effective. Regardless of the style of preparation, it should be made to appeal to the secondary school student and include such topics as the following:

1. Description of the physical plant
2. Administrative organization of the school

3. Student activities
4. Curricular offerings
5. Student regulations
6. Rules governing the use of lockers and the cafeteria
7. Student publications
8. Class schedules

Information Units or Classes. Information presented in a special class or as a unit within a regular class is the most effective technique. If information is presented in this manner, it has a definite allotment of time in the daily schedule, and the teachers are held responsible for the results of the activity. Such classes or units can be used as the core of the information service around which the other activities are planned. An information program which has a series of information units or special classes in the curriculum leaves little opportunity for major gaps.

The guidance staff can plan several different kinds of information units. The following types should prove most helpful:

1. A unit devoted to the occupational and educational outlets of a given academic subject. Example – a review of the occupational and training opportunities of those interested in vocations related to biology.
2. A series of units in a subject area. Example – a six-week unit on self-understanding in the seventh-grade social studies class; a six-week unit on the world of work in the eighth-grade social studies class; and a four-week unit devoted to integrating the two and drafting a high school plan in the ninth-grade social studies class.
3. A group guidance class of one or more semesters in length. The exact content of such a class will vary according to the information needs of the total program, but the following outline prepared by Leland Dean for a class in Buchanan High School, Buchanan, Michigan, is an excellent illustration of the content of the group guidance class.[4]
    1. My school
    2. What Good is High School?
    3. What Makes You As You Are?
    4. My Abilities

[4]Reproduced through the courtesy of Leland W. Dean.

5. Solving My Problems
6. How Important Are Grades?
7. How to Study More Effectively
8. What Is School Spirit?
9. Learning to be Likeable
10. Understanding Parents
11. Courtesy and Etiquette
12. Boy and Girl Relationships
13. Managing Money
14. Leisure Time Activities
15. My Personal Goals

The guidance staff may wish to obtain workbooks and special pamphlets for the information class or unit. A variety are now available through commercial publishers. Many schools prefer to develop their own units or course outlines and supplementary materials which are designed to meet local needs.

working with groups

One of the major problems in using group procedures in guidance is the difficulty that school administrators have in finding guidance personnel who are sufficiently trained in group dynamics. Groups of immature children are very often unable to operate in a permissive atmosphere, and well-trained teachers must be found who can switch roles regularly from that of leader to that of follower and back to being a leader again so that the group can maintain its effectiveness as a device for enhancing the growth and development of each of its members. Teachers and counselors who plan to provide guidance services to children in groups will be more effective if they remember that:

1. Groups vary in their unique characteristics as much as the individuals who compose them and should be treated accordingly.
2. Rather than destroy the individual pupil, the group should give every member an opportunity to increase his potential by capitalizing on the strengths of his personality and avoiding his weaknesses.
3. There are many different kinds of leadership roles to be assumed by the members of the group from time to time, and every participant should be given the opportunity to

hold a leadership position when he has a contribution to make to the group.

4. Before a group can be productive each of its members must feel that he is accepted by, and responsible to, the group.
5. The group should be composed of children enough alike to guarantee that they hold a common objective which can be clearly defined.
6. A method of operating that is informal and permissive allows each member a maximum opportunity to assume the role that he wishes to play, depending upon his interests and abilities.
7. Active participation by all members of the group insures stimulation to keep the group energized and moving toward its objective.[5]

Much more could be written about the sources and techniques of presenting information. It is hoped that the guidance staff will be able to provide the secondary-school student with at least the minimum information program from suggestions made here. Once the program has been started, the school staff should make every effort to supplement the foregoing suggestions through more research, creativeness, and effort. The ultimate goal is to help every student make intelligent choices based on a good background of significant information.

summary

In order to make the best possible adjustment to his environment, the secondary school student needs certain kinds of occupational, educational, and personal-social information. The information service makes available that information of special interest to individual students which is not ordinarily taught in the regular classes. Each stage in the process of maturing brings forth questions for which the student must find answers. The secondary school which dedicates itself to the task of assisting each student in rising to the maximum of his potential must be prepared to furnish unique kinds of accurate, up-to-date information. This aspect of the guidance program is the function of the information service.

---

[5]Raymond N. Hatch and James W. Costar. *Guidance Services in the Elementary School.* Wm. C. Brown Company Publishers, 1961, pp. 30-31.

A tremendous amount of occupational, educational, and personal-social information is now available from both commercial and noncommercial publishers. A wide variety of movies, stripfilms, and other audio-visual materials specifically developed for secondary school guidance programs can be rented at little or no cost to the school. The number of effective ways in which this information can be presented to secondary school students is limited only by the experience and imagination of the guidance worker.

selected readings

Baer, Max F. and Roeber, Edward C. *Occupational Information.* Revised Edition, Chicago: Science Research Associates, Inc., 1958.

Bennett, Margaret E. *Guidance and Counseling in Groups.* New York: McGraw-Hill Book Company, Inc., 1963.

Forrester, Gertrude. *Methods of Vocational Guidance.* Boston: D. C. Heath and Company, 1951.

Glanz, Edward C. *Groups in Guidance.* Boston: Allyn and Bacon, Inc., 1962.

Guidance in the Curriculum. 1955 Yearbook of the Association for Supervision and Curriculum Development. Washington, D. C.: National Education Association.

Hoppock, Robert. *Occupational Information.* New York: McGraw-Hill Book Company, Inc., 1957.

Houghton, Hubert W. and Munson, Harold L. *Organizing Orientation Activities.* Chicago: Science Research Associates, Inc., 1956.

Lifton, Walter M. *Working With Groups.* New York: John Wiley and Sons, Inc., 1961.

Kelley, Janet A. *Guidance and Curriculum.* Englewood Cliffs, New Jersey: Prentice-Hall, Inc., 1955.

Munson, Harold L. *How to Set Up a Guidance Unit.* Chicago: Science Research Associates, Inc., 1957.

Norris, Willa, Zeran, Franklin R. and Hatch, Raymond N. *The Information Service in Guidance – Occupational, Educational and Social.* Chicago: Rand McNally and Company, 1960.

Roe, Anne. *The Psychology of Occupations.* New York: John Wiley and Sons, 1956.

Super, Donald E. *The Psychology of Careers.* New York: Harper and Brothers, 1957.

Warters, Jane. *Group Guidance.* New York: McGraw-Hill Book Company, Inc., 1960.

Willey, Roy D. and Strong, W. Melvin. *Group Procedures in Guidance.* New York: Harper and Brothers, 1957.

Unit 5

The Counseling Service

In order to help each student reach the maximum of his potential, there are times when he must be worked with individually. Counseling with individual students is the interpretation, analysis, and planning aspect of the guidance program. Instruction, student activities, and school philosophy affect more students than does counseling, but personal counseling provides the only means whereby each student can become intimately acquainted with himself and his relationship with his environment.

A counseling service implies the presence of at least one person with training and time for counseling. It also implies a planned program for aiding students both through direct contact with the counselor and through contacts with teachers acting in auxiliary counseling roles. In the remainder of this chapter counseling is discussed primarily as an activity of a trained counselor, but ways in which teachers can contribute are also pointed out. The combination of teacher and counselor is regarded as the counseling service.

the nature and purposes of counseling

MAJOR PURPOSE OF COUNSELING

The purposes of counseling are many; indeed, the specific functions of counseling are nearly as numerous and varied as the students who present themselves to counselors. Nevertheless, a rather simple main purpose can be stated.

The major aim of counseling is self-understanding and, through self understanding, self-realization involving an awareness and acceptance of social responsibility.

This first purpose is much more complex in application than it might at first appear. It means that counseling is not only a learning process, but it facilitates the learning process. The counselor continually keeps in mind the long-term development of the counselee, for, even though counseling with an individual is not always carried on over a long period of time, decisions made during counseling will often affect the individual's future development from that time on.

Counseling is an individualized service, but it should be emphasized that counseling services exist for all students and not just those with deep seated problems. Obviously, then, counseling is not an isolated activity but an integral part of the total school program which utilizes the entire staff.

counseling activities

Although counselors may become involved in many outside activities, their most important duties are those related to the actual process of counseling with a student. Counseling proceeds largely through interviews in which the counselor is:

1. Obtaining information
2. Giving information
3. Interpreting
4. Engaged in therapy

The first of these, *obtaining information,* is usually carried out in preparation for counseling. Interviews which are for the sole purpose of obtaining information are not common with school counselors, although they are well known to employment interviewers and intake interviewers in institutions and psychiatric clinics. More often the counselor will find that initial interviews which concentrate too heavily on acquiring information interfere with subsequent conferences with the student. Whereas the employment interviewer is primarily concerned with obtaining sufficient information to make his own decision regarding the employment of the interviewee, and the intake interviewer is usually obtaining information to be turned over to a caseworker, psychologist, or psychiatrist, the school counselor is most concerned with establishing the rapport which is necessary for a continuing relationship. Information not obtained during the initial interview usually comes out in later ones and in a more meaningful context. By such means obtaining information becomes an integral part of the counseling process.

The second of the before-stated activities, *giving information,* is an important though sometimes discounted and maligned aspect of counseling. Giving information may be the most important and the only necessary step in dealing with some students who seek help from a counselor. Information requests can be classified as two rather different types:

1. Factual information about school regulations, requirements, vocational information, college entrance requirements, and the like
2. Personal data aimed at encouraging more realistic self-appraisal

The first concerns information about the characteristics of the external world; the second concerns information about the individual himself. These two often merge in the counseling process, but there is justification for looking at them separately. When a student comes to a counselor for specific information, this may be all he wants or needs at that particular moment. Some requests for information will only be a preliminary step to more extensive counseling, but this should not become the basis for assuming that all students requesting information are to be detained for additional counseling.

In handling a request for factual information, the counselor should keep the following points in mind:

1. He should accept the request as being important to the student – however trivial it may seem to the counselor.
2. He may need to assist the student in clarifying the nature of the request. Thus a request for information about entrance requirements of the state university may need further clarification, since the various departments usually have different requirements. Such clarification often results in a desire on the part of the student for extensive vocational counseling.
3. He may have to admit that he does not know the answer to the question the counselee has raised. If the counselor cannot at the moment give precise information, this admis-

sion should be made. Students can get vague generalizations and faulty information many places; from the counselor they should obtain correct and specific answers. If the counselor does not possess certain information, he should help the student find a suitable reference or another person who can supply the necessary information.

4. He should give the student an opportunity to indicate whether the information supplied really satisfies his need. It is easy, when busy, to fall into the habit of giving a brusque answer which often unsatisfactorily terminates the interview.

A request for factual information is superficially a simple one, yet the nature of a counselor's response will determine to a considerable extent the reputation of the counseling service which he offers.

The second type of request for information involves a search for self-knowledge. The student may be seeking the answers to such questions as:

Why is it that other people don't like me?
What is my I. Q.?
Do I have the ability to be an engineer?
How can I find out what I'm interested in?
Why do I have to spend so much time studying?

This type of question – while information-seeking in form – is of a different order than the factual information type previously discussed. The answers – despite student desires to the contrary – are not simple, and although they may involve facts, they are not truly factual. This type, however, does imply that more extensive counseling is being sought. The need for counseling arises out of two factors:

1. Questions of this type usually involve a depth of emotional involvement. Acceptance of the answer is a more complicated matter than in the former case and developing a program of action based on this acceptance will also be difficult.
2. The answers to questions of this type are so complicated that many types of information must be drawn upon. Assembling such data and presenting it to the student becomes a major task in interpretation.

Thus, both interpretation and some degree of therapy are involved in providing a completely satisfying answer to questions involving self-knowledge and understanding.

Interpretation, as a counseling activity, usually is the result of an attempt to give information to students in a meaningful way. Such interpretation can and does become very complex as the sources of information multiply. Reviewing each significant item from a cumulative record with a student might involve an expenditure of considerable time and still not be satisfactory, for meaningful interpretation requires that some synthesis be accomplished. The record folder by its very nature enforces some organizing of information, but the organization or synthesis undertaken in counseling must be related to the student's problem. If a student is considering the vocational alternatives of accounting and engineering, an initial synthesis of information can organize data into categories providing evidence of general intelligence, clerical aptitude, mechanical aptitude, interests, and experiences related to the two occupations. The requirements of the two fields can then be compared with the individual's profile.

The counselor is faced with another phase of interpretation which merges with the therapeutic process. This involves the interpretation of the individual's behavior or reactions. Such interpretations are aimed at helping the individual understand the reasons for his actions and how they appear to others. These interpretations should be made with care for they can be quite unacceptable to the student and thereby jeopardize the counseling relationship.

The fourth activity in counseling is that of *therapy.* The use of the term "therapy" needs some explanation. One viewpoint restricts the practice of therapy to treatment conducted by a psychiatrist or to those working under psychiatric supervision. Therapy is used here in an extended sense to include counseling activities chosen to help the student eliminate or alleviate concern he may have about some problem. Therapy may include giving information and making interpretations, but these are only part of a therapeutic relationship. Usually therapy involves several contacts, for the resolution of conflicts and the development of new attitudes and viewpoints are not quickly accomplished. Further attention will be given to this in discussing techniques used in the counseling interview.

elements of the counseling relationship

Counseling begins with the establishment of a personal relationship which will vary somewhat from counselee to counselee. There must be mutual respect and acceptance existing between counselor and counselee. There must be a willingness to give help on the part of the counselor and a willingness to receive it on the part of the student. These are necessary elements of the personal relationship or rapport upon which counseling is to be based.

Counseling of any significance cannot be done in the presence of others or in a place where there is excessive noise and many interruptions. As a minimum the counselor should have a private office. It should be comfortably and generally less formally furnished than the average office. It should be possible, when desired, to eliminate the "across-the-desk' approach to counseling. The less cluttered the office, the more the counselee can focus his attention on the problem and feel that he and his problem are important to the counselor. Sufficient time must also be available. The counselor who is loaded with administrative and clerical details may be so rushed that counseling interviews are conducted under pressure— one eye on the clock and the other on the counselee. Much of what a counselor accomplishes depends on his ability to place the concerns of the counselee ahead of everything else during the counseling interview. For some counselees this experience is in itself the most important element of therapy in that it restores a sense of self-worth and dignity. Space, time, and above all, the atmosphere established by the personal relationship, are vital to counseling.

Counseling should be aimed at facilitating the counselee's own efforts to resolve his problem. The counselor who perceives or thinks he perceives a solution to the problem being discussed will need a full measure of self-restraint if he is to avoid imposing it – however subtly – on the counselee. There is always the possibility that the counselor's solution is not the appropriate one or, if it is, that the counselee will not be ready to accept that particular solution. Of course, this concern with facilitation of the counselee's own efforts can be carried to an extreme. Individuals who have been highly dependent will not become independent merely because a counselor refuses to offer advice. In such cases the person is more likely to avoid a decision or to accept one from a friend, rela-

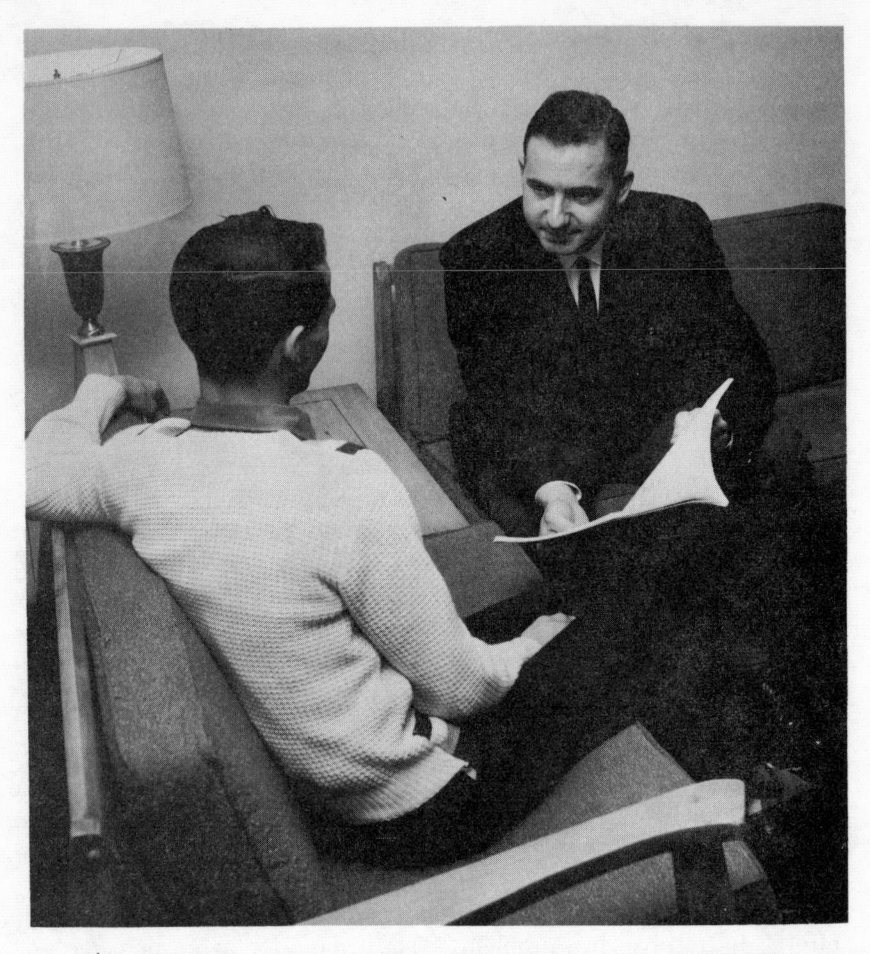

AN INFORMAL OFFICE ARRANGEMENT HELPS THE COUNSELOR CREATE A FRIENDLY ATMOSPHERE.

tive, or anyone else who will tell him what to do. Self-reliance is a long-term counseling goal and not a miraculous result of someone's having stepped into a counselor's office. Effective counseling sometimes involves the initiation of a new dependence relationship as a basis for developing independence.

The counselor must give attention to the counselee's total adjustment. An algebra teacher can teach an individual how to solve equations without concerning himself very much about how that skill will affect his social life or his sense of values, but the counselor has no subject-matter emphasis to excuse or to encourage such neglect. At times the counselor may be under some pressures from teachers or administrators to encourage greater conformity on the part of an individual student without much consideration of the implications of conformity for that student. The counselor may be requested by the student himself to condone certain behavior or to intercede for special privileges which yield temporary satisfaction but contribute to poor adjustment in the long run. Supporting such requests is not good for the counselor's reputation with other faculty members, and usually it is bad for the total adjustment of the student. The counselor's obligation is to see and to help the student see the broad and long-term implications of each decision.

The counselor should not assume that all of his obligations are fulfilled through his face-to-face contacts wtih counselees. Some cases require follow-up contacts with teachers, parents, or others who have personal contact with a given student in order to assist them in understanding the student's problems and the approach which may be most effective in working with him. Another aspect of follow-up is checking on individuals who have been counseled to determine whether the counseling was successful. Failure to do so is apt to mean that the counselor will fall into routine unimaginative practices with little insight into the actual effect these practices have on the individual.

COUNSELING ROLE OF THE TEACHING STAFF

Most guidance programs attempt to involve the classroom teacher in counseling activities. There certainly is much that the teacher can and should do, including:

1. Collecting information about pupils for the counselor and for the cumulative record folder.
2. Focusing instruction on student needs.
3. Modifying classroom relationship with certain students.
4. Exploiting friendly contacts with individual students.
5. Becoming an expert in certain types of vocational information such as the entrance requirements of a particular college or occupation.

The first of these functions has been dealt with in Units Two and Three. The only additional point to be made here is that the teacher should be included in the counseling service so that reporting information will be seen by him as an essential aspect of this phase of the guidance program. The other functions listed will help to develop this viewpoint. Functions 2 and 3 are interrelated but differ in emphasis. The *focusing of instruction* on student needs involves an awareness of the common problems faced by students and a conscious attempt to teach in these areas in order to be of maximum assistance. For example, all high school students are concerned about the selection of a vocation. A teacher of any subject can, by assignments, discussions, and the use of appropriate vocational information material, help students see the significance of that subject as a background for future work in a number of different fields.

The *modification of the classroom relationship* with certain students goes a step beyond the preceding function. Students who need additional encouragement to participate in a class discussion will be unobtrusively given that encouragement. Students who are afflicted with stage fright may be passed over for a time on oral recitation but gradually encouraged to make brief contributions. Considerable tact is required in such matters; obvious "babying" of individuals may disrupt class morale, injure the status of the individual with his group, and actually interfere with his progress.

Every teacher will find that closer relationships are more easily established with some students than with others. Whenever this is so, the teacher should *exploit the friendly contact with the student* in order to learn more about him and to mobilize resources to help him. This rapport can be utilized to make an effective referral to the counselor, or, after conferring with the counselor, the teacher can assume a counseling role. Coaches and vocational teachers, such as those in the fields of shop, home economics, and agriculture, often find such relationships developing with students because of the nature of their class activities. Students who have not been doing well in academic work may find great satisfaction in shop or athletics. A teacher who is sensitive to this and quick to recognize and appreciate the efforts of some students to build a strong friendly relationship with him will be an asset to the counseling service.

Teachers in vocational subjects always are expected to be *ready sources of information about vocations* to which their classwork is related. They are also aware of further training possibilities available in their particular fields, both locally and regionally. Teachers of the more academic subjects also should become experts on the important vocations related to their subject matter fields. The mathematics teacher might reasonably be expected to know more about the job requirements for the statistical, actuarial, and engineering fields than other teachers. Teachers in a school usually represent in their training a number of different colleges and universities. If each teacher undertakes the task of keeping up to date on the educational requirements and programs of the institution he attended, more exact information will be available to students than when a single counselor attempts to describe or evaluate all colleges.

It is apparent that the teaching staff can play a vital role in the counseling service, whether or not all of the teachers undertake specific counseling assignments. Interpreted in the broadest sense, all teachers do some counseling. Most teachers, however, do not have the psychological background, knowledge of standardized tests, experience in counseling techniques, or the time required for counseling in any but the least complicated cases. Hence, except in case of absolute necessity, it is unwise to depend solely on the full-time teaching faculty for provision of the counseling service. At least one qualified person should be available to coordinate the counseling efforts of teachers and to deal with all but the routine problems.

TEACHER PREPARATION FOR GUIDANCE[1]

Those who hold the concept that "every teacher is a counselor" often overlook the fact that counseling, whether done by a full-time or part-time person, should be done by only a well trained counselor. There is faulty logic in assuming that a half-time counselor needs only half the training. More and more teachers are becoming active in guidance programs as counselors and in other capacities. The teacher, in order to become an effective guidance worker, must acquire certain basic skills. Some of the more important ones are listed here.

LEARNING ABOUT PUPILS

1. The guidance worker must obtain sufficient training in the use of standardized tests to become well acquainted with

[1]Adapted from Raymond N. Hatch and James W. Costar. *Guidance Services in the Elementary School.* Dubuque, Iowa: Wm. C. Brown Company Publishers, 1961.

the wide variety of instruments that are available at the secondary school level and the proper techniques of interpreting test results to pupils and parents.
2. The guidance worker at the secondary school level should also become competent in the use of the most appropriate non-testing techniques for gathering information about pupils such as observations, autobiographies, and sociograms.
3. He should acquaint himself with the most appropriate methods for reporting and recording information about pupils.

PROVIDING OCCUPATIONAL AND EDUCATIONAL INFORMATION

1. The teacher in the high school planning to participate in the guidance program should be well acquainted with the various theories related to vocational choice and their implications for children of secondary school age.
2. He should be familiar with a wide variety of occupational information that is appropriate and available for secondary school children and the best methods of disseminating such information.
3. The high school teacher should be well informed about community guidance resources which can be used by the school to help youngsters become better informed about the world of work and the most efficient means for utilizing these resources.

COUNSELING WITH PUPILS AND PARENTS

1. Anyone planning to counsel with individual pupils should first obtain some actual interviewing experience with youngsters at this age level under close supervision.
2. It is important for the classroom teacher at the secondary school level to become acquainted with the purposes and procedures for providing guidance services to pupils in groups.
3. The high school guidance worker must be capable of conducting effective interviews with parents as well as children.

ADMINISTERING GUIDANCE SERVICES

1. The secondary teacher who plans to participate in the guidance program should obtain a thorough understanding of the

basic philosophy of guidance, and the recommended procedures for organizing and administering guidance services, in order to be more effective in coordinating the guidance services for the pupils in his classes and in order to serve on various faculty advisory committees set up to implement the program.

2. He must be sufficiently aware of the techniques of research and evaluation which are useful in helping the teaching staff evaluate the curricular offerings and instructional methods being used.
3. Every guidance worker should be familiar with the best procedures for making a good psychological referral, the agencies in the community that provide services to children, and the legal and ethical implications of working with agencies outside the school.

some points of view about counseling

TYPES OF COUNSELING RELATIONSHIPS

There is a wide range of contacts between two individuals which may involve some of the characteristics of counseling. This gives rise to argument about the kind of relationship desirable in counseling and to some feeling that the services of a trained or experienced counselor are not particularly superior to those of any other person. When looking at several levels of contacts, some of the distinctions among them become more apparent.

Friendly informal contacts or conversations between teachers and students are a familiar type of relationship. These contacts usually are not generated for any particular purpose, although students may — as we all do — use them to discuss or even dramatize their problems. The suggestions or advice which may be offered by a teacher under such congenial circumstances is not always taken seriously at that time. These contacts are beneficial primarily to students because of the democratic permissive atmosphere which they tend to create, and they are no less valuable to the teacher for the same reason.

A slightly more formal level of contact is that of a short interview on a particular problem. A student having difficulty with mathematics may seek help from his mathematics teacher, which results in a tutoring session on one or more troublesome exercises.

This hardly qualifies as a counseling session under ordinary definitions of counseling. However, such a session may open up issues regarding previous unsatisfactory experiences with mathematics, poor aptitude, or derogatory opinions of the value of mathematics expressed at home. Each of these issues might be so dealt with in a single contact that the student returns to his mathematics class with a considerably different outlook. Teachers dealing with students in this way are engaging in counseling at a rather simple level.

Many problems presented by students will require several contacts before they reach a satisfactory termination. Two to six contacts might be regarded as a "short-contact case," and this category will cover the majority of the counseling cases at the secondary level. The problems posed will be mainly of vocational or academic origin but with social and emotional overtones which often result in a type of counseling which is more than a purely intellectual approach. Attention to the reaction of the individual (and his associates) to proposed solutions may be the major factor resulting in extended contacts. However, for a student waivering between several vocational possibilities, the assembly of the necessary personal data, occupational information, and related material, and the analysis of these data with the student may also require several sessions.

Obviously the dichotomy between short-contact cases defined as involving up to six interviews and prolonged contact cases involving more than six interviews is an arbitrary one, as is any distinction based primarily on the number of contacts. The number is not necessarily proportional to the seriousness of the problem, but prolonged contact cases in a secondary school setting usually do involve some type of therapy. The home situation, for example, may be very unsatisfactory, and if nothing can be done about it, the solution probably lies in obtaining independence. Until this status can be achieved, the individual needs a friendly, receptive, but not overly sympathetic listener. In other cases, where the basic problem might again originate in the home, the difficulty may clearly lie with the counselee. This might be understood and even accepted after several interviews. However, continued contacts over a period of time may be necessary before new attitudes and viewpoints can be "fixed" to the point where they will result in altered behavior. This latter aspect of counseling is the one which has been designated here as therapeutic.

As an adjunct to a school counseling program, there is a need for special clinical services. Such services are included in the broad definition of pupil personnel services and include remedial work in speech, reading, and hearing; medical services; and diagnostic and psychiatric services for the more difficult cases. Normal individuals with problems commonly can be handled by teachers and school counselors, but when the problem becomes an abnormality in the individual, more specialized personnel are needed. Much of what transpires in such clinical services is closely akin to counseling and at some points is indistinguishable, but additional techniques and resources, which are not available to most school counselors, often are used by these clinicians.

RESPONSIBILITIES OF THE COUNSELOR

Certain issues of an ethical nature confront the individual who engages in counseling. The counselor has a primary responsibility to the counselee, but he also has a responsibility to the school administration and to society. Conflicts often develop among these responsibilities, and there may be cases where the order of importance is difficult to determine. A question may be raised as to why a counselor is in any different position than an ordinary teacher. Certainly good taste and common sense should govern the actions of both. The teacher who gossips about unusual bits of information that he has is flouting his professional responsibility. However, if a student confesses to a teacher that he broke into the school safe, he probably does so with the expectation that this will be reported. The teacher may be chosen simply because the initial confession is more easily made to a friendly person. The counselor, however, by assumption of that title, indicates to the counselee that his statements will be regarded as confidential. If the counselor shows irresponsibility in this regard, contact will be cut off with other students having certain types of problems and his value to students as a counselor will be negated. The counselor operating in a situation where he feels he must make formal reports to other individuals should make this clear to the counselee. As long as the situation is clearly defined beforehand, no confidences are broken. Regarding the example of the confession of theft, the counselor might be more hesitant about reporting the confession. The student will very likely come to the point of making a full confession to the proper authorities, particularly if given some encouragement by the counselor. However, if the individual refuses to make this open confession, the counselor must review his responsibility, recognizing that a confession is not proof of the deed and that false confessions are by no means uncommon. It then becomes primarily a question of which would be of greater benefit to the counselee — to report the confession or refrain from doing so for the time being.

The counselor repeatedly faces this problem of confidential information in dealing with teachers who wish to help a student. They would like to have pertinent information, yet may destroy rapport between the counselee and counselor by letting the student know that they have the information. Administrators and others concerned with disciplinary matters ordinarily would like to have access to confidential information to expedite their action and decisions. There are three courses of action possible:

1. Refusal to divulge any information — this ignores the fact that the counseling service has certain obligations to the school staff, and it is unrealistic in that such aloofness will in time reduce the necessary support for the service.
2. Information will be divulged but only by prior agreement with and permission from the counselee.
3. Suggestions can be offered as to how to deal with the student without giving the reasons for the recommendations. This may serve in cases which the preferred second alternative is ruled out.

Finally, the nature of these problems points up the responsibility of the counselor in providing leadership in guidance and related inservice training. As teachers and administrators more fully comprehend what is involved, the issues just discussed will become less significant.

APPROACHES TO COUNSELING

In recent years there has been much discussion of an approach to counseling called the non-directive approach. Any brief statement of the fundamental precepts of this viewpoint will err by oversimplification. However, emphasis is placed on the principle that the individual has within him the ability to change or to solve his own problems. The task of the counselor is less that of advising or interpreting and more that of accepting, reflecting, and clarifying.

The characteristics of the non-directive viewpoint are in contrast to a school of thought described as *directive*. The role of the directive counselor – taking an extreme position – is that of assembling information about the counselee from records and by interviewing, prescribing tests, and analyzing personal data with the ultimate goal of knowing enough about the counselee to recommend and even persuade him to a certain course of action. Probably few counselors have been quite as prescriptive as implied by this description, but undoubtedly many counselors are more directive than is desirable.

Few high school counselors – considering the pressure of time and the wide range of activities in which they are involved – can afford to adopt a consistently non-directive approach even if that were desirable. Their counseling should always be centered on the client, but the technique, in order to be most appropriate, can be *eclectic,* drawing from several points of view. Two of the authors[2] in a previous book listed ten major assumptions which describe the latter approach:

1. That an individual may or may not have the ability to analyze his problem or make realistic plans.
2. That an interview implies a mutual responsibility for diagnosis and planning.
3. That both participants have a responsibility for the outcomes.
4. That the results of the counseling process will be directly related to the relationship established between the two participants.
5. That the active participation of both individuals usually results in a more complete analysis and more valid plans.
6. That the counselee must be an active participant in order to accept the product of the process.
7. That no two interviews or interviewees are alike, thus it is necessary to alter the interview emphasis for maximum results.
8. That it is the responsibility of the counselor to provide those conditions under which all pertinent information will be brought to light for careful analysis.

---

[2]Hatch and Costar, op. cit., p. 136.

9. That resolving the counselee's problems or concerns is the major purpose of the interview, and therefore every interview should be closed only after the next step to be taken has been clearly defined.
10. That both participants recognize and accept the responsibility of the counselee to make the final decision from the alternatives which become apparent during the process of co-analysis.

COUNSELEE BEHAVIOR IN SUCCESSFUL COUNSELING

Generally speaking, the problems and concerns of adolescents often stem from inaccurate perceptions they hold of themselves (faulty self-concepts) or their environment (faulty information). In the case of the latter, teachers and counselors have for some time felt that helping a student develop a clear understanding of the opportunities in and demands of his environment is a major guidance activity. It is only in recent years that secondary school counselors have come to feel that they also have an important role to play in helping each student develop an accurate, positive self-concept that will facilitate the maximum development of his potential as a human being. A youth whose concept of himself is faulty or one of low regard cannot be expected to make the maximum use of his opportunities while in school. In fact, his self-concept can have considerable effect upon counseling itself.

The counselor who seeks to conduct his counseling with constant attention to its effect on the counselee should keep in mind four major steps characterizing the counselee's behavior. First, the counselee finds a discrepancy between his desires and his actual situation; in short, he wants something he does not have. Second, as a result of counseling, the counselee sees himself and his situation in a new light. Third, the counselee acts in accord with his new perceptions. And, fourth, he finds his action satisfying. If not, the process is repeated.

Counseling can hardly be successful unless the counselee really wants a change and wants it badly enough to make some effort to achieve it. If a student is in some way referred to a counselor and has not yet realized his need for counseling, the counselor's first task becomes that of arousing an awareness of need. The second stage is a key one in the counseling process. Unless the counselee develops new insights, it is unlikely that any benefit will result. It is for this reason that highly directive or prescriptive counseling is apt to be unsuccessful. The counselee's new perceptions are insufficient. He must make some plans and carry them out. While the counselor can assist by taking steps to modify the counselee's environment, this procedure carried to the extreme is inadvisable. Neither the counselor nor anyone else can follow an individual through life, smoothing his path and prevailing on others to make allowances for his deficiencies. Satisfaction with his behavior is based more on his own standards for evaluation than upon an evaluation of his behavior by others. The counselor who consistently looks for these phases in the client's behavior will thereby keep his counseling centered on the needs and the development of the counselee.

conducting the counseling interview

The counseling interview, as has been mentioned, focuses on the needs and desires of the counselee. The interview must be, to a large extent, characterized by permissiveness and acceptance. The direction taken by the interview must be guided by the interviewee or at least determined by his apparent needs and concerns.

PHASES OF THE INTERVIEW

The phases of the interview correspond rather closely to the essential elements of counseling discussed earlier. The first stage of a successful counseling interview, preparation, takes place prior to the interview itself. Preparation includes a review of information available about the prospective counselee and attention to the interview setting. Scanning the cumulative folder of a student may give the counselor some feeling of knowing the counselee and some clues as to how the interview might be conducted. This background should expedite rather than direct the interview and give the student confidence in the counselor. The importance of the interview setting in giving the counselee a feeling of acceptance, of well-being and relaxation, has already been noted.

Careful preparation is the first step in the establishment of rapport. Hatch and Costar[3] have suggested a number of techniques for the second step, that of helping to establish a good personal relationship with the counselee:

---

[3]Hatch and Costar, op. cit., p. 139.

1. Whenever possible rise to meet a pupil coming to your office for an interview.
2. Greet the child in a professional but friendly manner, and address him by name.
3. If he is a mature youngster, offering to shake hands may help put him at ease.
4. It is often advisable to use a "warm-up" topic as an opener with a child who finds it difficult to carry on a conversation with an adult. This topic should be of a noncontroversial nature or the relationship may be set back at the very beginning of the interview. Topics to avoid are religion, labor, politics, and others of a similar nature.
5. Give the youngster your undivided attention.

These suggestions are helpful points to keep in mind, but no mechanical attention to details will attain the rapport necessary for effective counseling. Sensitivity and patience on the part of the counselor are necessary. When these preliminary stages are complete and rapport has been established, the counselee will usually indicate it by presenting his problem – which may be by this time somewhat different from that implied in earlier remarks.

This introduces the third stage of most interviews, analysis. It is at this point that real counseling begins and the maximum of skill must be exerted. The counselee begins to identify and analyze those factors which he feels are related to the problem. The counselor listens not only for what is said, but for subtle clues revealed by tone of voice, gestures, hesitation, and the like. The counselor can expedite the process through the use of well-chosen comments, but he should be careful to encourage analysis by the counselee and not himself. At various points and certainly at the end of the initial presentation, the counselor will want to make a summary statement which will demonstrate his understanding of the problem and give the counselee an opportunity to clarify points which have been misunderstood. After correct understanding has been reached regarding the nature of the problem, the counselor may take the lead by raising questions which seem likely to further explain the situation.

The next stage of the interviewing procedure involves planning. In the early stages of counseling, planning may be directed toward further analysis of the problem rather than toward a solution. The possibility of taking tests, of utilizing vocational information materials, and of contacting other individuals are typical alternatives which can be selected in planning further interviews. If additional interviews are involved, specific plans should be made for at least the next one, and the counselee should be given a chance to discuss the number of interviews and the time lapse between them.

As additional information is brought forth and successfully analyzed, the counseling will move ahead to decisions or actions by the counselee which will help resolve the original problem. Some or all of the alternatives may have been examined before, but now they must be made more explicit. The counselee should be encouraged to propose action programs, and the counselor can propose still others for consideration. Counseling then becomes a process of examining the implications of each course of action and reaching a decision as to the most appropriate one.

Just as the first step in conducting a successful interview takes place before the interview, the last step, follow-up, takes place after the conversation has ended. This, like the preceding, is a step in each interview, but its nature may change somewhat as counseling progresses. One part of the follow-up is the recording of the major points discussed in the interview. A statement of the problem and the related facts noting conflicting data should be written up. Tentative plans and data needed for the next interview should also be noted.

In some cases both the counselor and the counselee have made commitments to be fulfilled by the time of the next interview. Some indication should be made of such agreements, and the counselor should take immediate steps to carry out his obligation. Failure to fulfill an obligation may destroy the effectiveness of further counseling because it conveys to the counselee a feeling that he is unimportant in the eyes of the counselor.

SPECIFIC TECHNIQUES IN INTERVIEWING

Conducting a counseling interview requires experience as well as ability. The statements made by a counselor may, through the choice of words and tone, aim at accomplishing any of several things. To encourage the counselee in presenting his problem, the counselor can simply recognize or accept what the student has said by a nod of the head or similar gesture. He might reflect both the content and the overtones of a statement in order that the counselee can further examine the full implication of his own remarks.

The counselor can interpret the significance of the counselee's reactions and experiences or relate them in new and more meaningful ways for the counselee. Such interpretations are usually a step toward helping the student develop new insights and put them to work. At times the remarks of the counselee seem to request reassurance, sympathy, or approval. The latter should be used sparingly, although there are occasions that do justify their use. At other times the counselor may feel that it is appropriate to make specific suggestions for activity between interviews. Examples would be reading, writing an autobiography, obtaining certain information, or seeking out a new experience.

Silence – even if it means biting one's tongue – is a technique which has great value provided, of course, that the general demeanor of the counselor indicates sincere interest in the counselee. To interrupt the thinking or talking of a counselee serves only to slow the progress of the interview. Humor, anecdotes, or personal references occasionally may find a place in counseling, but considerable judgment should be employed in introducing them. They may lighten a tense situation or help in achieving rapport, but they can also relegate the major purpose of the interview to a position of less significance. Threats, irony, sarcasm, or anything that may seem to imply rejection should be studiously avoided.

The counselor must not be obvious in applying these various techniques. He should feel comfortable in the use of that technique which seems most appropriate at the time. He must also be sensitive to how his statements sound to others. Recording interviews with play-back for self-criticism or criticism by other counselors is a very effective procedure for developing an awareness of one's own interviewing techniques.

some typical problems and the counselor's approach

POOR SCHOLARSHIP

Unsatisfactory grades represent one of the most frequent problems that occur at the secondary level. Teachers, parents, and school administrators often place such emphasis on grades that students with low marks are subject to reprimand and mandatory referral to the counselor. Since the primary objective of the guidance program is to help each youngster rise to the maximum of his potential, poor scholarship is of great interest to the counselor.

SELF-EVALUATION IS AN IMPORTANT PROFESSIONAL ACTIVITY ENGAGED IN BY SCHOOL COUNSELORS.

Every underachiever is an indication that the school has not been able to reach this objective.

In preparing for an interview with a student referred for poor grades the counselor will want to examine the cumulative record, seeking answers to the following questions:

1. Has the student a long history of low grades or is this a recent development?
2. Do the low grades have any relationship to evidence of the student's ability, reading skills, and interests?
3. Are the student's grades generally consistent with his ability?
4. Has the student recently chosen a school curriculum or a pattern of courses which is too difficult for him? Is there a program which might be more suitable?
5. Have there been any recent disturbing events in the life of the student?
6. What is known about the parental attitude toward education generally and grades specifically?

7. Are brothers or sisters currently enrolled in school and what is their pattern of grades?

Each of these questions may have an answer which will help to explain the situation, but unless the counselor already knows a great deal about the student, he will do well to regard the answers as only tentative.

The underachiever – the student whose grades are below what his ability level would indicate – has usually been told this repeatedly. He may, in fact, take some pride in the fact that he is unusual in this respect and that people "just don't understand why his grades are so poor." The implication of this is that the counselor should be cautious about making statements of what should be expected from the student in the way of grades. The first thing to ascertain is whether the student is concerned about his grades and, secondly, whether he sees any discrepancy between his grades and his later goals. School is not ordinarily a pleasant place for a person with low grades; and any lack of concern – if real – suggests that the indifference may be caused by preoccupation with other problems. If one or more such problems can be brought to the surface, counseling can proceed on a more fundamental basis than if grades alone are the point of attack.

Remedial work in reading, arithmetic, or study skills, a change in curriculum, or a change in vocational plans may overcome low grades in certain areas if they are of recent development. They are somewhat less likely to work any great improvement where the pattern of underachievement has existed for several years.

The result of counseling with students having low grades can be one or more of the following:

1. Improved grades through more work or a change of program.
2. Adjustment of vocational and educational plans to a continuing pattern of low grades.
3. Acceptance as satisfactory by parents of performance previously regarded as unsatisfactory.
4. Withdrawal from school (age permitting) or a cooperative work-study program.

For the most part successful counseling should result in improved grades, but this is not always an expected or desirable outcome.

EDUCATIONAL AND VOCATIONAL PLANNING

For some years most of the guidance and counseling activity was educational and vocational in nature. Some counselors persist even yet in orienting themselves almost entirely to vocational guidance and thereby assign themselves a less significant role than counselors are entitled to have. However, in a school situation a counselor can expect to find that most of his counseling is with students presenting problems of an educational or vocational nature. The counselor should be aware of two factors in dealing with these problems:

1. Educational or vocational problems frequently represent the basis upon which a student chooses to approach a counselor even though he has another more pressing concern.
2. Educational and vocational planning, because of its relation to such things as parental hopes or expectations, college attendance, marriage, and military service, may have many emotional involvements which are varied and intense.

In preparing for an interview with a student when the problem is presumed to be that of educational or vocational planning, a counselor will want to review the cumulative record with particular attention to:

1. Level of ability
2. Interest patterns – measured and stated
3. Aptitude patterns
4. Previously stated plans

If the test data are recent, perhaps no additional testing will be necessary. If not, the counselor can tentatively note that some additional testing may be appropriate during the first interview – providing it still seems desirable after the most immediate concerns of the student have been ascertained.

As the interview progresses, the need for additional test information, occupational information, and college admission requirements may become apparent. Plans should be worked out to acquire these data and to analyze their significance. At this point a difficult situation often arises since students and parents would like to have some assurance of success in a chosen vocation. This is difficult to give. After going through all of the statistical terminology in prediction, the essential thing for a counselor to keep in mind is that few predictive data have definite meaning for a given individual. Even if 99 out of 100 with a certain score on a test have failed in the past, the counselee may feel that he is 1 in 100. Educational and employment opportunities permitting, he is entitled to take that chance if he wishes to do so.

In addition to an extensive vocational information file, the counselor should establish those personal contacts which will enable him to arrange for interviews for students wanting firsthand information about jobs. Such interviews have considerable educational value in addition to the occupational information they provide. Personal contacts with business and industry also expedite placement.

The problems of educational planning in high school are gradually being lessened by the modification of college admission requirements. No longer is the student who fails to take mathematics in the ninth and tenth grade, or four years of English, automatically barred from college. He may, however, be limited in the number and type of colleges he can attend. Planning the student's secondary school educational program is not so momentous an event as it once was, but students and parents are not yet fully aware of this. Perhaps the wisest counsel in educational planning is to keep the student's program as flexible as possible while covering all the alternatives one can.

ANXIETY AND PERSONAL ADJUSTMENT

It is in the area of anxiety and personal adjustment that some of the most serious counseling difficulties arise. This is also the area where most counselors are likely, with good reason, to feel least competent. There are a number of professional groups such as clinical psychologists, psychiatrists, psychiatric social workers, and psychoanalysts who are inclined to regard this area as assigned to their particular discipline. The school counselor, many of these specialists contend, should restrict himself to dealing only with educational and vocational problems and refer immediately those cases with personality involvements. The issue is a difficult one to resolve, for distinctions between educational and vocational problems on the one hand and psychoneuroses on the other are more easily made on paper than in practice. Furthermore, many schools and communities lack referral facilities, and the expense of private treatment would be a burden for most families. Hence, counselors are sometimes forced to continue working with students whom they would rather refer elsewhere. The more severe mental disorders (psychoses) which demand hospitalization usually include such extreme symptoms that quick action can be expected from the parents to remove the child from school for treatment. It is the less severe "neurotic" type that is most apt to cause difficulty for the counselor. This type of student is well enough to be in school but profits less from it than most of his classmates.

The counselor who detects phobias, muscle tics, obsessions, abnormal sex interests, hallucinations, or delusions will want to consider immediate referral to a clinic or specialist. Irritability, pervasive anxiety, difficulty in concentrating, and oversensitivity are symptomatic of general tension which may demand extended and "deep" therapy. Many of these symptoms can exist to some degree in normal individuals, but in their extreme or combined forms are likely to indicate an abnormality of serious proportions. It may be an organic disorder, and such a possibility must be checked at once. The error most likely to be made by the inexperienced counselor is that of attempting to deal with the symptoms themselves, a procedure seldom of real value and fraught with danger because new and more serious symptoms may appear to replace the old ones as long as the basic problem still exists.

With such cautions in mind, the counselor still must be prepared to deal with students referred to them because of "poor personal adjustment." In such cases, particularly, the cumulative record should be reviewed for evidence of (1) unusual or improper behavior; (2) social contacts and group affiliations; (3) state of health; (4) instability (economic or emotional) in the family; and (5) concern, worry, or general anxiety. By so doing, the counselor may be alerted to factors suggesting a major difficulty calling for more than usual care in dealing with the student.

In handling emotional and adjustment problems, it is advisable to consider whether the problem arises out of specific environmental conditions over which the individual has little control or whether the unsatisfactory situations are a result of factors within the individual. In the latter case, the counselee is likely to be disturbed about many situations because his personal deficiencies interfere with everything he tries to do.

The typical student troubled by an environmental situation can be helped either to see it differently or to deal with it differently. The techniques by which these ends can be accomplished have already been presented in the discussion of interviewing. If, as counseling continues, no noticeable progress is made or the anxieties of the individual appear more diffuse and pervasive, it is probable that counseling oriented to the immediate situation is inadequate. In all likelihood, the individual requires a fundamental restructuring of his personality — the development of a different set of attitudes — which involves long-term therapy that few secondary school counselors have the time or ability to provide.

evaluating the counseling process

A totally adequate plan for evaluating counseling is difficult to devise. Even at the university level, the amount of high quality research completed in this area is limited. It can hardly be expected that secondary school counselors will be able to perform a task that has been so inadequately done by researchers with more time, money, and training. Nevertheless, the conscientious counselor will seek evidence of his effectiveness and, more important, seek means of improvement. There are a number of factors that the high school counselor should be constantly weighing.

SATISFACTION OF THE COUNSELEES

Satisfaction on the part of those counseled is not necessarily an indication of effective counseling, but general dissatisfaction on the part of many counselees is a good indication that the counselor has been unsuccessful. Follow-up interviews several months after counseling provide one index of satisfaction, although a highly biased one if the original counselor conducts the interview. A simple questionnaire or check list which preserves the anonymity of the respondent is a somewhat more objective indication of satisfaction. Reactions of teachers regarding the behavior of the student after counseling or the reactions of teachers to suggestions made to them by the counselor for working with the student are other evidences of satisfaction. Interviews with parents may also be helpful in this endeavor.

IMPROVEMENT IN GRADES

Many cases handled by a counselor deal with unsatisfactory grades or with indefinite educational or vocational plans. In such cases, we have noted that grades will generally improve after successful counseling. This is not a universally desirable goal, but it is a tangible and objective outcome.

ADHERENCE TO PLANS

If plans laid in counseling are appropriate, it is to be expected that most counselees will be following them several months or a year later. It should also be true that students who have been adequately counseled will show less vacillation thereafter than students who have not received satisfactory counseling. The cumulative record system should provide ready evidence of this sort.

BEHAVIORAL CHANGES

When personal and social adjustment are involved, it is to be expected that some changes in behavior will result. It has already been pointed out that teachers' statements regarding student behavior indicate an awareness of and some degree of satisfaction with the outcomes of counseling. Anecdotal records, if consistently reported, can be compared with earlier ones to see what changes are apparent. Detailed case studies of a sample of counseled individuals will help show the success or failure of counseling. An expert consultant may be asked to review a number of cases and react to the way they were handled.

RECORDING OF INTERVIEWS

The playing back of one's recorded interviews with students will frequently point out faulty counseling techniques. A sequence of recorded interviews on the same student will indicate whether changes are taking place in the student during counseling. It also points out more clearly how economically the interview time is being used. One very simple check is that of determining how much of the time the counselor speaks as against how much of the time the counselee speaks. If the counselor consistently talks over half the time, he will do well to review and revise his tactics. Occasionally another counselor, or the entire counseling staff, should be asked to listen to one's recording and comment critically on it.

STATISTICAL EVIDENCE

Such simple evidence as the number of students seen each month, the per cent of the student body seen in a year, the average number of interviews per student, or the tabulation of the reasons for coming to the counselor give some indication of what the counselor is accomplishing. There are no absolutes for comparison, but a counselor who sees only a small proportion of the students will want to study the reasons for this. If almost all his contacts involve but one interview, there is the possibility that his counseling may be superficial or unsatisfactory to the students. If more students come in on their own or by referral from other students, the situation is vastly better than if the counselor has to call them in or deal largely with referrals by teachers.

Evaluation, as just suggested, will help the counselor improve himself professionally and provide him with a more adequate basis for interpreting to others what he is doing. The temptation, often because of the great need for counseling in most schools, to spend most of one's time seeing students and dealing with records, jeopardizes the quality and the future of the counseling service.

summary

In order to profit the most from his school experiences the student often needs help in making a satisfactory adjustment to his environment. The efforts of the school to assist students in making this adjustment are carried out primarily through the counseling service. A counseling service must make use of all staff members, teachers and administrators as well as counselors, if the service is to be successful.

As long as human beings differ as they do, there necessarily must be more than one approach to counseling. Techniques used by one counselor are often inappropriate for another. The same is true for approaches used with clients. Whichever the approach, the critical element in successful counseling is the interpersonal relationship that exists between the counselor and the student. It is this relationship, built upon mutual respect and acceptance, that makes counseling the most meaningful personal experience a student can have and the heart of the guidance program.

selected readings

Arbuckle, Dugald S. *Counseling: An Introduction.* Boston: Allyn and Bacon, Inc., 1961.

Buchheimer, Arnold and Balogh, Sara Carter. *The Counseling Relationship: A Casebook.* Chicago: Science Research Associates, Inc., 1961.

Cottle, William C. and Downie, N. M. *Procedures and Preparation for Counseling.* Englewood Cliffs, New Jersey: Prentice-Hall, Inc., 1960.

Loughary, John W. *Counseling in Secondary Schools: A Frame of Reference.* New York: Harper and Brothers, Publishers, 1961.

Marzolf, Stanley S. *Psychological Diagnosis and Counseling in the Schools.* New York: Henry Holt and Company, 1956.

McGowan, John F. and Schmidt, Lyle D. *Counseling: Readings in Theory and Practice.* New York: Holt, Rinehart and Winston, Inc., 1962.

McKinney, Fred. *Counseling for Personal Adjustment in Schools and Colleges.* Boston: Houghton Mifflin Company, 1958.

Patterson, C. H. *Counseling and Psychotherapy: Theory and Practice.* New York: Harper and Brothers, Publishers, 1959.

Rogers, Carl R. *Client-Centered Therapy.* Boston: Houghton Mifflin Company, 1951.

Stout, Irving W. and Langdon, Grace. *Parent-Teacher Relationships.* Washington, D. C.: Department of Classroom Teachers, National Education Association, 1958.

Tolbert, E. L. *Introduction to Counseling.* New York: McGraw-Hill Book Company, 1959.

Tyler, Leona E. *The Work of the Counselor.* Second Edition. New York: Appleton-Century-Crofts, Inc., 1961.

Unit **6**

Placement and the Follow-up and Evaluation Services

The utilization of guidance services with an individual student follows a logical sequence. The inventory and information services are concerned with gathering personal and environmental information as it pertains to each student. The counseling service is responsible for assisting him with the interpretation and assimilation of such information in order to help him develop his own unique aptitudes and interests to the maximum of his potential. To make the best use of what he has learned, the student then needs help in getting suitably placed at the next step in his educational program or on a job. The organized effort of the school to provide assistance with the latter is the placement service. After the former student has spent some time in the new setting in which he has been placed, he is then in a position to compare and evaluate his school experiences and offer suggestions to the school for improvement of the training of future students. The collection of information about and from former students is the follow-up and evaluation service. Techniques for conducting the placement and the follow-up and evaluation services are discussed in this Unit.

the placement service

The placement service is responsible for assisting all students in taking their "next step," whether it be to a job, to a school for advanced training, to an apprenticeship program, or to a part-time job while in high school. The machinery to carry out this responsibility may be located in several areas of the school program, but all of the aforementioned activities must be in operation if the school is to have a complete placement service.

The placement service can be organized in one of several ways. It may be:

1. A *decentralized* plan in which the various departments and individual staff members all are responsible for the placement of students in all types of situations.
2. A *centralized* plan in which all placement activities of the school are handled through one individual or office.
3. A *combination* of the two plans.

In a given situation any one of the patterns might be the most desirable; however, the most efficient structure for a majority of the schools seems to be the *centralized* plan. The centralized pattern provides a main office to which all employers can turn for service; it treats all students in a more unbiased manner; it makes maximum use of the most completely trained placement personnel; it reduces duplication and competition from within the school; and it encourages improved cooperation with private and public placement agencies. A word of caution relative to centralized placement should be expressed here. As a rule, certain staff members of the school have job contacts which only these staff members are able to maintain. Provision must be made in the centralized plan to utilize the contribution of all such people in order to insure greater service to the majority of students. The centralized pattern should not be thought of as a service to be offered by a few, but rather as a central coordinating office through which the efforts of all staff members can be channeled for the greatest efficiency.

Many school administrators are opposed to a school placement service, maintaining that other public placement offices are now rendering the service, and the school would be duplicating their efforts. Valid though this line of reasoning may sound, the guidance staff is obligated to raise the following questions:

1. Is there a free public placement service in the immediate vicinity?
2. Is the public placement service caring for the training aspect of placement?
3. Does the public placement service offer a complete and satisfactory part-time job service?

4. Does the public placement service have, or can it obtain, better personal data than that available from the school files?
5. Can the public placement service interpret the true qualifications of the student to the prospective employer in such a way as to prevent the employer from criticizing the school for certain gaps in the employee's training?

If the answers to these questions are in the negative, then the school has no other course than to develop its own placement service to meet the obligation of improving student adjustment. It should be pointed out, however, that cooperation between the school and public placement services is to be encouraged, for in this manner both agencies will render greater and more efficient service to more students and employers at less cost.

STEPS IN DEVELOPING THE PLACEMENT SERVICE

First Step. The first step in the development of the secondary school placement service is *identification of staff* to render the service. A number of characteristics should be considered in nominating an individual to direct the placement work. The following are important criteria for use in making the selection:

1. Personnel training and experience
2. A knowledge of the community and a wide acquaintanceship with people in the community
3. Work experience other than teaching
4. Experience as a counselor or as an active guidance worker in the school
5. Acceptance by other staff members and students
6. Desire for administrative responsibility
7. Familiarity with the philosophy and objectives of the senior high school
8. Knowledge of child labor laws

Second Step. The second step in implementing the placement service is that of providing *adequate housing.* At the outset, the office space for the service should not be pretentious, but allowance should be made for a few minimum essentials. For most situations the following items should prove adequate:

1. Telephone
2. Desk and chair

3. Card file
4. Book shelves
5. Typewriter and desk or table
6. Additional furniture to accommodate a part or full-time staff member

The housing for the placement service should be located with several considerations in mind:

1. Near the cumulative records
2. Near the center of student traffic
3. Easily accessible from the street
4. Near the counseling offices
5. Near the offices of the coordinators if a cooperative work program is offered

Third Step. The third step in the new placement program is that of *determining the scope of the initial service.* Schools have tried several different approaches to the problem, utilizing one or more of the following:

1. A survey of student job and training needs
2. A survey of placement opportunities in the community
3. An analysis of all placement work now being done in the school
4. A survey of opinions and suggestions from parents and prospective employers

From the results of one or more of these approaches, the first phases of the placement service can be established. As a general rule, part-time employment and the details for placement in training institutions are logical aspects to develop first in the program. This is because of the heavy demand for service which results when a complete placement service is announced and because the job placement aspect is usually a slow-developing phase. Job placement may be even slower while the placement director works out the details of cooperation, with the public and private placement agencies.

Fourth Step. The fourth step in the development of the placement program is that of *preparing the necessary forms and records.* It is at this point that the placement services must be developed specifically for the local situation. Certain basic information usually is common to all placement work and with that in mind, a number of suggested forms are included here as samples.

PART-TIME RECORDS

A file of students interested in part-time employment to broaden their school experiences is the first essential in offering a placement service of this type. A suggested form which the student should complete is shown in Figure 8. The space on the back of the card can be used to record the work record of the student. This record should be very helpful for later referrals, but if a report of work performance is obtained from the employer, the record will have even greater significance. A suggested form which the employer may use to report such performance can be found in Figure 9. An explanation of the meaning of the terms in the rating scale should be helpful to the employer and increase the validity of the ratings.

EDUCATIONAL RECORDS

Each year more secondary school students make applications for admission to institutions of higher learning. In addition to this trend, more students are seeking other types of training after graduation from high school. A parallel development has been an increased appreciation, on the part of the training agencies, for information about the student's secondary school experiences. The impact of these two conditions on the principal of the secondary school has resulted in a tremendous increase in the demand for his services. More and more, the administrator's time is being consumed with the preparation of information blanks for the various schools, colleges, or universities. The principal has frequently delegated this chore to others, and in some cases he has set up an educational placement office to deal with the problem. The latter approach seems to be a logical solution to the problem faced by the principal, but it does not reduce the amount of work demanded of the school staff.

Schools have tried many ways of reducing the work load brought about by the rapid increase in demand for student information. Some schools charge a fee for all blanks completed after the first; others make up a basic set of data on each student and mail it to the institutions to which the application has been made. In both cases, one or both parties involved are not satisfied with the result; the student tends to resent the fee charged to obtain information about himself and the college authorities seldom are satisfied with a standardized set of data about the student. The obvious answer would be for the secondary schools and the colleges to agree on certain basic information about each student. This still seems to be in the remote future

Placement Office

APPLICATION FOR PART TIME WORK

PRINT—Last   First   Middle   Birthdate   Class

Address   Phone   Date

CHECK HOURS YOU DESIRE TO WORK

	8	9	10	11	12	1	2	3	4	5	6	7	8	
Mon.														
Tues.														
Wed.														
Thurs.														
Fri.														
Sat.														
Sun.														

Check (XX) Work in which experienced.

Check (X) Work you are willing to do.

........Butcher
........Store Clerk
........Library
........Shorthand
........Typing
........Bookkeeping
........Canvasser
........Baby Sitting
........House Cleaning
Others (list)
....
....

........Helper in Private Family
........Janitor
........Business Machines
........Manual Labor
........Waiter-Waitress
........Bus Boy (Meals and Wages)
........Carpenter
........Yard Work
....
....

Figure 8

EMPLOYER RECORD

Student's Name ____
Last First Middle

After the student leaves your employment, please complete this card and return it to the placement office.

(Company)

RATING SCALE

Please Check Appropriate Block	Work Performance	Cooperation	Punctuality	Appearance	Attitude
Outstanding					
Above Average					
Average					
Below Average					
Weak					

ADDITIONAL COMMENT

Type of Work

Date Signature of employer

Figure 9

so the secondary school must take the necessary steps to improve its service to students while keeping the work load from becoming prohibitive.

For the individual or individuals responsible for educational placement there are several ways to reduce the work involved in preparing data blanks for training institutions. The following steps should ease the burden:

1. Survey the student body to obtain the names of all youngsters considering applications to other training institutions.
2. Obtain certain basic information about each of these students at least one semester before they are to leave.
3. Develop a file of such information in such a way that a clerk can type from the blanks. (This is a digest of the more detailed information of the cumulative record).
4. Reserve only that information which is confidential for completion at the time the application is to be mailed.

The crux of the foregoing plan rests in the forms used to collect the basic data. Such forms must include all the information typical of most college applications, and at the same time be only an abstract of the information in the cumulative record. Forms of this kind can be prepared for the local schools or for a number of adjacent schools. A series of three forms is suggested here which may be of value to those who are planning to prepare forms of this type. The forms are Personal Data (Figure 10), Academic Data (Figure 11) and Confidential Data (Figure 12). The first two can be completed by the clerical staff from the cumulative record and the third by the counselor or other qualified persons. The three forms can be clipped together and filed alphabetically, ready for immediate use when applications are requested.

JOB PLACEMENT FORMS

There is a wide variation in the exact format of the forms used for job placement. The variation in most cases is justified by the particular needs of a given institution. In spite of the differences which are to be found in forms now in use, certain basic types are common in most placement activities. The four types which are most popular are:

1. Prospective Applicant
2. Notice to Prospective Applicant (in duplicate)

Educational Placement
Personal Data

1. Name in full ______________________________ Date __________
(Last) (First) (Middle)
2. Permanent home address ______________________________
(Number and Street) (City) (State) (Phone)
3. Mailing address ______________________________
(If different from home address) (No. and Street) (City) (State) (Last date you will be here)
4. Birthplace __________ Date of birth __________ Are you a U. S. citizen? __________
Month Day Year
5. Single ____ Married ____ Husband's or wife's full name __________
6. Have you had any experience in the Armed Forces? ___Yes ___No Total months in service ____ Branch of Service ____
7. Have you at any time applied for admission to any college or university? ____ If so, give name of the institution and full details of the outcome of your application __________

8. List in chronological order all high schools attended.

Name of Institution	City	State	Attendance Dates (Month and year)
			from to
			from to
			from to

9. When do you expect to enter college? ____Fall ____Winter ____Spring ____Summer. Year ____
10. a. (1) Father's full name: __________ (Last) (First)
Address __________
(If different from No. 2)
(2) Living? ____ (3) Is he a U. S. citizen? ____
(4) Occupation __________
10. b. (1) Mother's full name: __________ (Last) (First)
Address __________
(If different from No. 2)
(2) Living? ____ (3) Is she a U. S. citizen? ____
(4) Occupation __________
11. If you have a legal guardian or foster parents, give name __________
Address __________ Relationship to you __________
(Street and Number) (City and State)
12. Give names, addresses, and occupation of at least two responsible adult persons as references (not former teachers or relatives)

____
(Name) (Address) (Occupation)

Figure 10

Educational Placement
Academic Data

1. Student's name ....
Last First Middle

2. Date of graduation.....................Type of program followed by the applicant in your school (check one) ....College Preparatory Course ....Other..................
specify

3. Number of students in class..........Approximate rank in class from the top..........
(circle quartile rank) 1 2 3 4
Grade point average, Key (A-4), (B-3), (C-2), (D-1), (F-0) ....

4. Academic record of all subjects taken whether passed or failed. (Include present-omit mark)

Unit Value	Subjects	Marks	Unit Value	Subjects	Marks
	English—First Year			Agriculture	
	Second Year				
	Third Year				
	Fourth Year				
	Foreign Languages			Home Economics	
	Algebra—First Year				
	Second Year			Commercial	
	Geometry—Plane				
	Solid				
	Trigonometry				
				Industrial	
	Biology				
	Chemistry				
	Physics			Music	
	Social Studies				
	History—World			Other Subjects	
	European				
	U. S.				
	American Gov't.				
	Economics				

Figure 11

Educational Placement
Confidential Data

*Personal Characteristics	Poor	Below Average	Average	Above Average	Superior	Comment
Seriousness of purpose						
Independence of effort						
Emotional stability						
Social adjustment						
Integrity						
Maturity related to age						
School citizenship						
Probable success in college						

*Composite of all Ratings

Test Results:

Date Taken	Name and Form of Test	Norm

Additional information which will be of value to the college in understanding the student.
(To be completed by the Counselor)

Figure 12

3. Summary of Qualifications
4. Introduction and Follow-up

Typical forms which illustrate the above are to be found in Figures 13, 14, 15, and 16.

PROSPECTIVE APPLICANT

Mid-Town Public Schools
Placement Service

....	....	....
Name	Address	Telephone
....	....	....
Birthdate	Social Security Number	Sex

Type of Work Desired
(If more than one type, indicate 1st choice with a one, 2nd choice by two, etc.)

1.	6.	11. ....
2.	7.	12. ....
3.	8.	13. ....
4.	9.	14. ....
5.	10.	15. ....

Figure 13

The format, content, and number of placement forms can be altered to a considerable degree if the school has a close working relationship with a public placement agency. It is advisable to hold a number of planning meetings with representatives of the public placement agencies before the exact forms and methods of referral are determined.

The placement staff may wish to delay the preparation of the Prospective Applicant form until the demand for employees in certain types of work is ascertained. When such information is available, the type of work for which employees are sought can be printed on the cards. It is quite possible that several different cards will be required to meet the needs of broad categories of work. For example,

NOTICE TO PROSPECTIVE APPLICANTS
Mid-Town Public Schools
Placement Service

Name of Company	Date
Address	Time of Application
Apply to	Type of Contact
Specifications and Duties:	Name of Applicant
	No. of Openings—No. Recommended

Figure 14

it may be desirable to have a card for those interested in such areas as clerical work, sales, part-time jobs, and industrial work. In most placement offices, it is advisable to keep the number of cards at a minimum. Every effort should be made to develop a card which is sufficiently flexible to permit the filing of information about all applicants. The reverse side of this form can be used as a record of referrals and of previous work experience.

The Notice to Prospective Applicant form should be made in duplicate. The placement office should give the original copy to the applicant and retain the carbon copy as a record of referral. If a master record is kept of all placement referrals and the disposition of the referral, the carbon copy can be destroyed as soon as entry is made on the master sheet.

The information for the Qualifications form should be completed as soon as the student applies for work. Several copies of the data can be made at the same time and kept on file for immediate use in case of referral to several employers. Most of the information can be taken directly from the cumulative record with the possible excep-

SUMMARY OF QUALIFICATIONS

Mid-Town Public Schools
Placement Service

____
Date

Name	Birthdate	Address	Tel. No.

____
Sex

Occupation of: Father ______________
Mother ______________
Guardian ______________

Qualifications:

1. Scholastic Aptitude (use code) ______________
2. Academic Achievement (All subjects—use code) ______________
   Strongest Subject (use code) ______________
   Weakest Subject (use code) ______________
3. Co-curricular Achievements ______________
4. Summary of Ratings (Staff) (use code)
   a. Dependability ______________
   b. Accuracy ______________
   c. Initiative ______________
   d. Cooperation ______________
   e. Leadership ______________
   f. Personal Appearance ______________
   g. Cheerfulness ______________

(See Reverse Side)

Code: AA—Above Average
HA—High Average
A—Average
LA—Low Average
BA—Below Average
(of typical student)

Figure 15

INTRODUCTION AND FOLLOW-UP

Mid-Town Public Schools
Placement Service

Qualifications form attached ( )
Qualifications form will be mailed ( )

______________ Name of Prospective Employer ______________ Date

This is to introduce ______________ (Name of Student) who is being referred by this office in response to your request for applicants for ______________

______________ (Type of Work)

We appreciate the opportunity to suggest the names of individuals for possible employment in your organization. Will you please check the appropriate blank below, sign, and mail this card? Please destroy the Qualifications form.

This applicant was employed ( )

This applicant was not employed ( )

Reason: ______________

____
Representative

Figure 16

tion of the staff ratings. A duplicated sheet containing the student's name and the list of items can be used by the placement officer to collect the opinions of staff members best qualified to rate the particular student.

The back of the Qualifications form can be used by the placement officer to describe any pertinent information not specifically covered by the standard items. Special limitations or strengths the applicant may have for the job in question, unusual need or other extenuating circumstances, and the personal opinions of the placement officer are the kinds of information which might appear on the reverse side of the form.

If the Qualifications form is to be of much value, it should be received at the potential employer's office either before or as soon as the applicant arrives. If the form is mailed, it may not reach the employment office in time for consideration or it might be mislaid by the employer. To overcome this problem, it is desirable to place the form in a sealed envelope and attach it to the form used for introduction. The student should be cautioned that the envelope is not to be opened but given to the interviewer with the seal intact.

The Introduction and Follow-up form should be prepared on a common postal card and given to the student as a way of introducing himself to the personnel interviewer. The return address of the placement officer can be printed on a number of cards well in advance of their use in referral.

The mechanics for the utilization of the placement forms will vary according to the needs of the local school. The entire guidance staff should assist the placement officer in determining the exact procedures of operation. The forms and procedures mentioned here are suggested as guides to the school staff. Local experience and further investigation should be considered when preparing suitable forms and procedures of the placement service.

Fifth Step. The fifth step in the development of the placement service is that of *interpreting the service to the students, staff, and potential employers.* Interpreting procedures start before the service is offered and are maintained in some form at all times. The interpretation serves as a means of determining placement need, improving the service, and conveying the results. A placement service which neglects any one of the three general aspects is vulnerable to attack and possible liquidation in times of financial stress.

Many different approaches have been suggested for the public relations phase of placement work. Since the procedures are so varied and would require considerable space for inclusion, only a list of typical activities used for interpreting the program to the parents and the public is included here:

1. Reports to students, staff members, and employers concerning present placement activities.
2. Assembly meetings of students devoted to an explanation of the advantages and procedures of the newly created placement agency.
3. Letters to potential employers explaining the placement procedures planned by the school and including an invitation to avail themselves of the service.
4. School staff meetings to review the ways in which the staff can enhance the service.
5. Presentations of the service to all local service and social clubs.
6. Newspaper, radio, and television explanations of the mechanics and accomplishments of the program.
7. Explanations of annual reports of past activities of the service to all students, teachers, and employers.
8. Discussions of ways for improving the service with all interested individuals.

A guidance staff interested in providing a good placement service to the students must assume full responsibility for the successful completion of the five suggested steps. A placement program which does not include all five steps is of questionable value to the student, employer, and school. If placement is to be a service, then time, staff, and effort must be provided or the omissions will soon overshadow and negate the efforts of a limited service.

the follow-up and evaluation service

The *Follow-up and Evaluation Service* is a research service for the total school program. It is the service which concerns itself with the successes, failures, attitudes, and opinions of former students. As a general rule, it is applied to those students who have left the school either by graduation or termination prior to the completion of their work. It need not be confined to this narrow concept, for it may be thought of as any organized effort to ascertain similar information from former students of a given grade or school while they are still enrolled in the school system. For example, the elementary school staff may wish to follow-up last year's students who have enrolled in the junior high school. Regardless of the point or grade at which the information is to be collected, it provides the school with that information which makes the educational offering more meaningful for present and future students.

Various purposes for conducting follow-up studies have been suggested by many different authorities in the field. Most of the suggestions are quite similar if the kind of information sought is used as a basis for improving the curriculum and techniques of instruction. Examples of the various kinds of information which can be expected from follow-up studies are listed here:

1. Reasons given by drop-outs for leaving school prior to graduation.
2. Suggestions offered by drop-outs as to ways of increasing the school's holding power.
3. Kinds of problems faced by former students and the grade level at which these problems arose.
4. Present locations of former students with emphasis on both residence and employment.
5. Types of training taken by former students after they left the secondary school.
6. Changes which should be made in the curriculum to bring about maximum benefit for today's student.
7. Additions and deletions needed in the cocurricular activities.
8. Kinds of problems faced by students when they first left school and suggestions for overcoming these problems.
9. Weaknesses in present school and community relationships and suggestions for improvement.
10. Vocational data which can be used to describe local employment conditions.

STEPS IN DEVELOPING THE FOLLOW-UP STUDY

It is not difficult to obtain agreement among school staff members that the information gained from the follow-up study is of vital importance. The problem which is of most concern to them is that of implementing the study. Factors such as leadership, time for the study, method of sampling, and ways of reporting the information are the primary stumbling blocks. Again, the guidance worker must accept the premise that there is not just one way of doing the job. There may be several equally valid approaches. The suggestions which follow are based on this contention.

First Step. The first step in the development of a follow-up program is the *identification of staff* to give the work interested and qualified leadership. This is a service which may utilize staff members who are sufficiently motivated to carry on the work but lack the training and experience necessary for other guidance activities. If the guidance staff assumes the responsibility for explaining the role of the follow-up service and for leadership in implementing the activities, many teachers can make an invaluable contribution to the guidance program. The primary characteristic in selecting participants should be interest in doing the work. After interest has been determined, the guidance staff can furnish them with the reading materials and verbal explanations necessary for understanding the techniques to be used.

The organizational make up of the follow-up committee could include the following individuals:

1. The principal
2. A counselor
3. A teacher of English
4. A teacher of business education
5. A teacher of social studies
6. A teacher of science

The logical chairman of such a committee is the counselor. The teachers included on the committee are in a position to integrate many of the follow-up findings into their respective curriculums, and the principal, as an administrative officer, is in a strategic position to assist in implementing the study. Many schools work through groups and, therefore, have students represented on the coordinating committee. In those schools where an administrative officer is directly in charge of guidance work, he should be included on the committee as might others when the specific situation requires their assistance.

Second Step. The second step in the development of the follow-up study is to *determine the sample to be studied and the methods to be used.* The initial study usually sets a pattern which is followed for a number of years. Thus it is quite important to plan an extended program so that it will become a continuous service.

Several specific decisions must be made in selecting the initial sample. The following are typical questions which must be answered:

1. Should graduates, drop-outs, or both be contacted?
2. How long should former students have been out of school before being contacted?
3. Should all former students be contacted or just a sample of the total number?
4. What pattern of sampling should be established for future studies?

If the study is to include a wide breadth of valid information, both graduates and drop-outs should be surveyed. The study should also reflect both the opinions of students who are recent graduates and of those who have had considerable experience after school. Contacting individuals who have been out of school one, five, and ten years should reveal both kinds of information. If the typical school class consists of fewer than one hundred students, it is advisable to attempt to contact all of them. If the classes have more than one hundred, a sampling procedure may be equally effective. Valid sampling is extremely difficult. There are at least two methods in general use today:

1. Follow-up every class the first year after graduation.
2. Follow-up classes according to the one, five, and ten year plan, but study only a particular group every third year.

The method used in conducting the follow-up study usually includes questionnaires, personal interviews or a combination of the two approaches. The questionnaire is the method which requires the least time, but the interview method usually results in more valid responses. The combination method of a detailed questionnaire sent to the entire group and a structured interview with a selected sample seems to be most satisfactory, if enough interviewers are available to carry out the procedure. However, a detailed questionnaire with an appropriate introduction will usually be quite satisfactory. It must be recognized, however, that certain individuals are less prone to return questionnaires. Many of those who feel that they have done poorly in life, have certain resentments toward the school, or have been drop-outs may not report by the questionnaire method.

Third Step. The third step in carrying out a follow-up study is *the development of the necessary forms.* The main forms are the covering letter, interviewing form, and questionnaire. The covering letter should be brief and personalized. The questionnaire should provide space for brief and objective answers. If a structured interview is planned, the questions which the interviewer is to ask should have more space for the entry of longer answers. Examples of the first two forms are to be found in Figures 17 and 18.

COVERING LETTER

Mid-Town High School
Mid-Town, South Dakota

Mr. Henry Amis
620 Oak Street
Old Haven, Ohio

March 8, 1962

Dear Hank:

It has been five years since you donned cap and gown and bid farewell to Mid-Town High School. We hope that during these five years you have found use for the education you received while a student here. Some phases of the training have probably been more helpful to you than others. You may have wished for an opportunity to tell us how we could improve our school program, and now is your opportunity.

Attached is a questionnaire which we hope you will complete and return at your earliest convenience. You may wish to omit some of the items. Remember, the greater the number of questionnaires we get back and the more complete the information on each questionnaire, the easier it will be for us to make desirable changes in the school program.

The students and staff of Mid-Town High School join me in expressing our appreciation to you for assisting us with this project. We wish you success in the years ahead, and we hope you find it convenient to visit us in the near future.

Cordially yours,
J. J. Jones
Principal

Figure 17

The blank which is prepared for the interviews may include more items since it will be read and completed by the interviewer. The same general information can be obtained in the interview as

Mid-Town High School
Follow-up Questionnaire

1. Name .... Address ....
2. Are you single? .... Married? .... Divorced? .... Widowed? .... If married, when? ....
3. Name before marriage .... 4. Graduation class ....
5. If not a graduate:
   a. What grade were you in when you left school?
   b. Why did you leave? ....
....
....
6. If you have had additional training:
   a. Name of school attended ....
   b. Length of attendance ....
   c. Do you feel that you were adequately prepared for college? Yes .... No .... If not, why not? ....
....
7. How are you now occupied?
   a. .... Employed for wages, full time
   b. .... Employed for wages, part time
   c. .... Unemployed and seeking work
   d. .... Unemployed and not seeking work
   e. ...... In Armed Forces
   f. ...... Housewife
   g. ...... In school full time
   h. ..... Other ....
8. What regular jobs have you held since you left school?

Kind of work	Name and address of employer
a.	....
b.	....
c.	....
d.	....

9. How long a period of time elapsed between the end of your high school education and your first job? .... months.
10. How well are you satisfied with your present job?
    a. .... very satisfied
    b. .... somewhat dissatisfied
    d. ...... reasonably well satisfied
    e. ..... highly satisfied
11. In what way did you obtain your present position?
    a .... through family or friend
    b. .... public employment agency
    c. ...... private employment agency
    d. ...... school officials
    e. ...... newspaper
    f. ..... found it yourself
    g. .... other ....
12. To what extent has the counseling you received been helpful to you? (Counseling means help by teachers, counselors, and principals with educational, vocational, and social problems)
    a. ...... it wasn't helpful
    b. .... very little help
    c. .... some help
    d. ...... extremely helpful
13. What is the relationship of your high school training to your present job?
    a. ..... no relationship
    b. ...... it gave me some background
    c. ..... it gave me a good background
14. What courses do you feel were not offered in high school that should have been? ....
15. How could the school have served you better? ....
....
....
....

Figure 18

16. SUBJECTS: Check the five that have been most valuable and *number them in order of most value.* 1 2 3 4 5.

Algebra	Civics	Gen. Math.	Physics ....
Anc. History	Clothing	Gen. Science	Sol. Geom. ....
An'l Husbandry	Bus. Arith.	Gen. Shop	Spanish ....
Art	Driver Trng.	Geometry	Shorthand ....
Band	Economics	Glee Club	Trigonometry ....
Biology	English	Health	Typing ....
Bookkeeping	European History	Home & Health	U. S. History ....
Carpentry	Farm Crops	Mach. Shop	Woodshop ....
Chemistry	Farm Management	Mech. Drawing	
Chorus	Foods	Pen. & Spell.	

17. What high-school subjects have served you least?
18. Please indicate by checking in the proper column how much this school helped you in regard to each of the following:

	(1) A great deal	(2) Some	(3) Little or none	(4) Un-certain
Using your spare time				
Taking care of your health				
Taking part in community and civic affairs				
Marriage and family life				
Securing a job				
Getting along with other people				
Preparing for further education				
Understanding your abilities and interests				
Ability to read well				
Using good English				
Using basic math skills				
Using your money wisely				
Conducting your own business affairs				
Thinking through problems				

19. If you have further comments or suggestions for improving any part of this school's program, please state them here. ....
....
....

Figure 18 (Continued)

that gathered from the questionnaire. The guidance staff should try several pilot interviews before printing the exact items on the interview blank.

Many schools are using the postal card questionnaire for follow-up studies. This method seems to have the greatest value for the annual follow-up of all students. The limited amount of space restricts the amount of information obtained by this method, although the percentage of returns is usually higher than when the longer questionnaire is utilized.

Fourth Step. The fourth step in the development of the follow-up program is *the compilation of addresses of former students.* There does not seem to be an entirely effective way to accomplish this step. Various methods are used to keep the mailing lists up to date. The following are offered as suggestions:

1. Cooperate with the alumni association in the maintenance of a dual file.
2. Sponsor a contest for students currently enrolled and award prizes to the class or club submitting the greatest number of up-to-date alumni addresses.
3. Hold meetings with the graduating class and exit interviews with drop-outs to explain the purpose and value of the follow-up information.
4. Contact local direct-mail advertising agencies for the loan of mailing lists.
5. Ask each member of the junior class to keep in touch with one member of the senior class for one year after he graduates.
6. Send Christmas or birthday cards to graduates and drop-outs each year with a reminder for them to notify you of any changes in addresses.
7. Use the last address given by the student before leaving school. This is quite satisfactory for the recent school drop-out or graduate, but quite ineffective for those out of school from five to ten years.

Fifth Step. The fifth and last step in implementing the follow-up study is that of *tabulating and utilizing the results.* The completed questionnaires and interview blanks can be entered on a master sheet. One sheet should be devoted to each item, and the data should be entered as soon as the blanks are returned. The exact form and method of tabulation is governed by the content of the survey blank. This is a clerical task, and the information should first be entered verbatim from the blanks. If provisions have been made for identification of the respondents, reminders should be sent to those who have failed to return this questionnaire within the specified time. When the final deadline for returning the blanks has been reached, the follow-up committee can synthesize and analyze the results. A summary report of the findings should be prepared. The report should include the following:

1. Brief descriptions of the purposes and procedures of the study.
2. Simple tables of the responses to each item.
3. Conclusions and recommendations.

The function of the committee should be to increase the readability of the report through clear and concise interpretation.

The report should be distributed and discussed by several different groups. The students, staff, and the parents should all be informed of the implications of the study. The curriculum committees of the school should study the findings in detail. A student assembly meeting may be devoted to the survey. A parent-teacher or board of education meeting may be spent on the findings. Summary findings usually are appropriate for a newspaper, radio, or television story. Every effort should be made to see that the results of the research are brought to the attention of all interested individuals if the full impact of the study is to be utilized.

summary

In this unit it was pointed out that the placement and the follow-up and evaluation services fall into the logical sequence of guidance services provided to assist each student in rising to the highest level of his potential. Before he can get the most from his educational experiences, he must understand himself and be understood by his parents and the staff members who are working with him. It is the function of the pupil-inventory service to expedite the development of this understanding. The information service assists the student by providing the occupational, educational, and personal-social information which will enable him to choose wisely from the many alternatives in making his life plans. In order to overcome all the obstacles standing in the way of his development, there will be times when the student can profit from the opportunity to discuss his conflicts and concerns with a person who has the training to help him analyze the unique conditions under which he is personally operating and to draw valid conclusions. This is the function of the counseling service.

In this unit the placement and the follow-up and evaluation services were discussed. The placement service is designed to insure that the student will make the best possible use of what he has learned by helping him get suitably placed in a vocation or at the next level of his educational program. The placement service, whether organized on a centralized or decentralized basis, depends upon the aid and cooperation of the entire faculty.

The follow-up and evaluation service assists in the attempt to individualize the educational experiences of each student by collecting, analyzing, and reporting data from students which describe their impressions of the experiences they had at some grade level in the school. It includes their suggestions concerning curricular offerings, instructional techniques, the guidance program, and extraclass activities. Data is also collected by the guidance worker from other sources regarding the abilities, interests, needs, and concerns of the student body which will enable the faculty and administration to more accurately assess to what degree the total school program is meeting the needs of individual students.

selected readings

After High School, What? Chicago: Chicago Public Schools, Department of Instruction, Bureau of Pupil Personnel Services, 1960.

Andrews, Margaret E. *Providing School Placement Services.* Chicago: Science Research Associates, Inc., 1957.

Baer, Max F. and Roeber, Edward C. *Occupational Information.* Second Edition. Chicago: Science Research Associates, Inc., 1958.

Froehlich, Clifford P. *Guidance Services in Schools.* Second Edition. New York: McGraw-Hill Book Company, Inc., 1958.

Guide for Making a Follow-up Study of School Drop-outs and Graduates. Sacramento: California State Department of Education, Guidance Bulletin, No. 13, 1950.

Kitson, Harry D. and Newton, June B. *Helping People Find Jobs: How to Operate a Placement Office.* New York: Harper and Brothers, 1950.

Kleiner, Julius. "Some Techniques of Better Placement," *Personnel and Guidance Journal,* Vol. XXXIII (September, 1954), pp. 34-35.

Parten, Mildred B. *Surveys, Polls, and Samples: Practical Procedures.* New York: Harper and Brothers, 1950.

Reed, Anna Y. *Occupational Placement: Its History, Philosophies, Procedures, and Educational Implications.* Ithaca, New York: Cornell University Press, 1946.

Roeber, Edward C., Smith, Glenn E., and Erickson, Clifford E. Second Edition. *Organization and Administration of Guidance Services.* New York: McGraw-Hill Book Company, Inc., 1955.

Smith, Glenn E. *Principles and Practices of the Guidance Program.* New York: The MacMillan Company, 1951.

The Follow-Up Service. Guidance Staff. East Lansing, Michigan: College of Education, Michigan State University, 1960.

Unit 7

Implementing The Guidance Services

"How do we start?" is a common question today asked by educators convinced of the merit of the five guidance services. Future guidance workers deserve an answer to this realistic and natural query. Avoidance of the question creates doubt and uncertainty in their minds, but to propose an answer here before reviewing certain basic concepts may result in much misunderstanding, malpractice, and disillusionment. The following concepts should be clear in the minds of the school staff interested in starting a program of guidance services.

some concepts to be considered

RECOGNIZING PRESENT GUIDANCE PRACTICES

Many aspects of the guidance program usually can be found in the present school program. Current practices in the school need to be identified and brought to the attention of the entire staff, or the more enthusiastic teachers might assume that the guidance work they have done is considered of no consequence and withdraw from activity in the new plans.

CONVEYING THE NEED FOR GUIDANCE SERVICES

Basic to the implementation of any activity is the obvious requirement of creating a felt need in the staff and students. A school staff or student body which does not recognize the need for guidance services neither assists in developmental plans nor participates in the established program.

INFORMING THE ADMINISTRATORS

The school staff, as used here, includes individuals with both line and staff responsibilities. A majority of the teachers have only staff responsibility. If guidance activities are to be effective, they must be understood and accepted by the faculty members with line responsibilities as well. The best work and thinking of the teachers will accomplish nothing if the uninformed administrator does not cooperate.

LIMITING THE INITIAL SERVICES

A common mistake made by many guidance workers is that of starting too many activities at once and including every staff member. In the early stages of implementing a program, it is better, as a general rule, to start fewer services and involve only those individuals with a strong desire to participate. A few successfully completed guidance activities have a far greater impact on the favorable development of the guidance program than many activities only partially completed.

LISTENING TO STUDENTS

The guidance program exists primarily for the youngsters of the school. The expressions voiced by students as to what they feel are the guidance services most urgently needed can be a valuable source of direction in starting the program.

DEFINING GUIDANCE SERVICES

The "What and Why" of guidance are fundamental questions to be reviewed with all staff members. Unless the guidance services are clearly defined at the outset, the initial activities suggested for study may include every conceivable activity practiced by educators. It is extremely unfair to permit a well-meaning teacher to start an activity in the name of guidance work which is only remotely related to it, and then disregard the teacher's suggestions as not being pertinent to the subject.

possible steps of implementation

Many different ways have been suggested by various writers in the guidance literature for starting the guidance program. Seldom will the reader find a definite recommendation of the best approach to the problem. As a result, he is often prone to condemn the authors for what may appear to be evasiveness. Criticism of this kind is unfair and quite unrealistic, for no two school programs are alike, no two school staffs are the same, and most important, no two schools have the same student body. To expect a recipe for the organization of a program of guidance services when the differences are so marked is only wishful thinking. It would be better to investigate the various approaches, select the one which seems most appropriate, make the necessary adaptations for the local situation, and then develop a plan of action. Mistakes might be made in using this approach, but the program has a better chance of being successful if an analysis of the local situation is made before specific steps are undertaken.

In spite of the inherent dangers in suggesting a step-by-step approach for the implementation of a guidance program, the following steps are offered as a general guide. The suggestions are quite general, but they provide the local staff with an organizational framework from which a program of guidance services can be developed in most schools.

Step One – The school administrator and those staff members most interested in improving the guidance program should review the various ways of determining the need for guidance services.

Step Two – An interim committee should be appointed by the administrator to exercise leadership in further development of the guidance program.

Step Three – One or more of the following techniques should be employed with and/or by the entire staff:

1. A follow-up study
2. A case conference
3. A series of staff meetings devoted to the "What and Why" of guidance services
4. A staff analysis of present services
5. A student analysis of present services
6. A presentation of the results of one of the foregoing techniques to the entire faculty for discussion

Step Four – The specific activities or services to be implemented immediately should be designated. A discussion involving the entire staff of desirable next steps will assist the guidance committee in selecting appropriate activities and identify those staff members interested in implementing them.

Step Five – Near the end of the school year, the following three sub-steps should be taken:

A. Review and report to the staff the activities attempted during the year.
B. Solicit suggestions from the staff for next year's program.
C. Appoint a coordinating council to direct further development of the guidance program.

Step Six – Identify activities and personnel for the next year. If a preschool conference is held, plans should be made to utilize a part of the conference to interpret and review the activities which have been outlined for the new year.

techniques for clarifying the need

In Step Three of the foregoing outline, six different techniques are suggested for helping the staff to envision and appreciate the need for guidance services. The interim committee may use one or more of the techniques to develop an understanding on the part of the staff of the needs of students. In addition, the techniques should assist the staff in determining methods of approach and omissions in the present services. The more the staff participates in the application and interpretation of the results of the various techniques, the greater will be their acceptance of the guidance point of view.

Two of the six suggested techniques have been discussed at length in previous units of this book. The "what and why" of guidance services and the follow-up study are covered in Units One and Six respectively. Many different guidance tools and techniques, which can be used as a background for the application of the sixth technique, are discussed in Unit Two. One additional guidance technique not discussed in earlier units and other suggestions for enhancing staff readiness for the guidance program are reviewed here.

THE SCATTERGRAM

One of the techniques which is frequently used to help the staff develop an increased appreciation for the individual and his problems is the scattergram. It is a graphic means of showing the achievement of students in relation to their ability to do schoolwork. If each teacher makes one scattergram for her class followed by a faculty discussion of what the information means, much growth will take place. The discussion will lead to an explanation of the use of other kinds of student information and the probable effects of such data on the improvement of instruction. The teaching staff will be able to see a practical use for the information which should result in an increased interest in further investigations.

The data for the scattergram are easily abstracted from the cumulative record. Two areas of information are needed – scholastic aptitude and marks of achievement. The scholastic aptitude can be presented in any form, such as I.Q., percentile, or decile. The achievement factor may be in the form of marks, general estimates, or any relative scale which will show the teacher's estimates of the students' achievement.

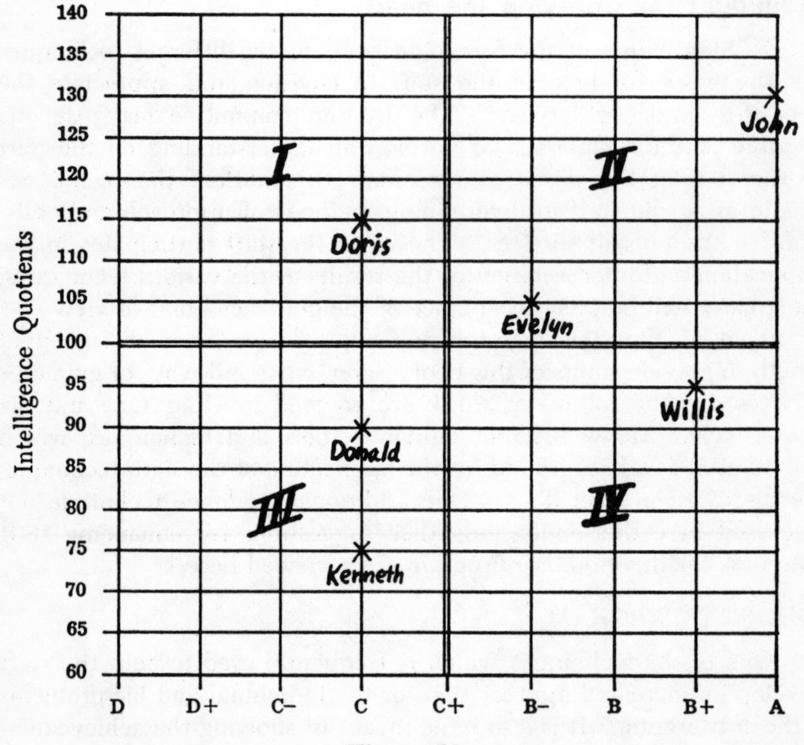

Figure 19

The scattergram is drawn as a square, which is divided into four major quadrants. The achievement estimates usually are indicated on the base line of the square from left to right starting with the lowest grade. The aptitude norms are then indicated on the left vertical line with the lowest score at the bottom. The averages of the two factors being compared are placed at the mid-point of the respective sides. Intermediate lines are usually drawn for each of the major increments of the factors being plotted.

To illustrate the scattergram, an example (Figure 19) is included here using only six students. Major intermediate lines have been indicated for the purpose of clarifying the presentation.

To determine the quadrant for each pupil, a point is marked where the lines representing the characteristics intersect on the scattergram. For example, Doris has an I.Q. of 115 and an achievement estimate of "C." The point at which these two lines intersect is the spot where her name, or a number which corresponds to her name, is placed.

Each quadrant represents a certain type of relationship in terms of the information used. Quadrant I contains the underachievers; Quadrant II, the high ability – high achievers; Quadrant III, the low ability – low achievers; and Quadrant IV, the overachievers. In this case Doris is an underachiever; Willis is an overachiever; and the others are performing as one would expect them to perform.

Many adaptations of the scattergram are used in presenting information, but the emphasis should be placed on a study of the findings rather than the finer points of plotting. In this illustration certain things are obvious: one student is an underachiever and one is an overachiever. What this means and what should be done with students of this type are points to be discussed. It is not always possible to find a definite method of working with each type, but a discussion will bring out many possibilities which teachers can share. An increased appreciation of what should be expected of each student, a deeper understanding of the effects of many factors on a student's accomplishment, and a greater familarity with the guidance services, both available and unavailable, are but a few of the outcomes of the use of this technique.

THE CASE CONFERENCE

The case conference has rapidly become one of the outstanding methods of training teachers to understand and appreciate pupil personnel work. This method has been used for many years in the training of social workers and clinical psychologists, but only recently have educators adopted it as an in-service technique. Although there are many different adaptations of the case conference, most of them follow the same general pattern. In most case conferences, all the faculty members immediately concerned with the student and his adjustment meet for the purpose of studying his needs. Each person is expected to add information so that all can profit by knowing the student from every angle. Each participant is expected to offer suggestions for the improved adjustment of the student. It is further expected that every participant will grow professionally in terms of the meaning of student information and the different types of action that might be taken.

Three different groups are usually represented in a case conference. The technique needs a *discussion* leader who is qualified to analyze the information available and to act as a consultant on some of the suggestions for action. If a visiting teacher, counselor, or psychologist is available in the school, he is the logical person to act in the leadership capacity. The second group is made up of those teachers who work with the student. This group can be called the *core group.* The third group is made up of other staff members who do not know the student, but who may add much to the discussion and profit from the activity. This group is called the *sounding board group.*

The number of participants in the case conference is a debatable issue. There are so many variables that it seems highly doubtful if an ideal number can be selected; however, minimum and maximum numbers can probably be arbitrarily established which should permit the greatest benefits for all staff participants. It would seem that the case conference technique, as described here, will need at least three and not over twelve participants if all are to contribute and profit from the ideas of others.

The conference can be thought of as having three major phases. The first phase is concerned with the collection of data for presentation. In the second phase the information is appraised and significant factors identified. Warters[1] calls this the "synthesizing" of information. The last step is the action step where both immediate and long term recommendations are made for helping the student.

---

[1]Warters, Jane. *High School Personnel Work Today.* New York: McGraw-Hill Company, Inc. 1946. pp. 64-66.

The type of case selected for study is of prime importance in the use of the case conference technique for in-service growth and staff development. It is not wise to choose the most difficult case, for the chances of showing good results in one year are small. The selection of the "model" student does not provide a sufficient challenge to keep the staff interested. Thus it would appear that a child with problems of adjustment, but not the school's "headache," would be most desirable. The underachiever, the unusually aggressive student, or the withdrawn student are good examples to be used for this type of case conference. For the reader who might find a previously prepared case helpful, the authors have included the *Case of Paul* in Appendix A, together with a series of related multiple-choice questions designed to bring forth a more comprehensive description of Paul by the staff.

COMBINING THE CASE STUDY AND CASE CONFERENCE

For purposes of illustration, the following steps are suggested as one way of conducting a case conference in a junior or senior high school. This is a combination of the case study and the case conference. It is rare, except for instructional purposes, that a case study will ever be completely developed by one person. More often the case study is the recording secretary's report of the case conference itself.

Participants:

Leader – The counselor
Core Group – Homeroom, mathematics, and physical education teachers and the principal
Sounding Board Group – The teachers of the freshman class

Step One – The core group selects the case to be studied.

Step Two – The leader, working with the core group, collects all available data about the student from the school records.

Step Three – The basic data are reproduced and the student's problem clearly stated.

Step Four – The first meeting of the series of conferences is held. The leader assumes the responsibility for:

1. Reminding the group of their responsibility for treating the information in a confidential manner.

2. Presenting the information on a duplicated sheet which can be distributed at this point and collected at the end of each meeting.
3. Calling on each of the core members to make corrections and add to the description of the pupil and his environment any pertinent data that has been omitted.

Step Five – All members of the group are encouraged to discuss the information and to identify the pertinent factors.

Step Six – Suggestions are made for steps to be taken in helping the student before the next monthly meeting.

Step Seven – All succeeding meetings start with a report of new information to be added, observed progress in the adjustment of the pupil, and an evaluation of the action already taken.

Step Eight – When the participants feel that further meetings about the case are no longer justified, a final evaluation meeting should be held. A complete review of the case, with a discussion of the relative value of the prognosis and therapeutic action taken during the study, is essential.

Step Nine – It is desirable to hold a meeting of the group one or two years later to review the progress of the case. However, excessive changes in personnel might make this impossible.

The school staff that takes the time to participate in a series of case conferences will be a much more effective staff. Many teachers will gain a new outlook on learning problems and a new appreciation for the individual and his mode of adjustment. They will have not only a new frame of reference, but they will also have new ideas extremely helpful to them in making their classroom work more meaningful to other students. Within this changed atmosphere, the student profits and that, of course, is the goal of all guidance activities.

STAFF ANALYSIS OF PRESENT SERVICES

Techniques for ascertaining the necessary scope of the guidance program and a method of analyzing present services can be combined into one device, the survey check list. The check list can be prepared by local staff members and might use a format consisting of the five guidance services. Additional items can be added to the list to cover the areas of administration and evaluation of the program. Normative data to determine the quality of a service will not be available, but each staff member has an opportunity to appraise the activities now in progress and to visualize the scope of a typical guidance program. Frequently the staff, while reviewing the results of the completed survey blanks, will find that guidance activities are being conducted by certain staff members, and until now these activities have been known only to a few.

The survey check list seems to function most effectively if it is prepared and distributed to the entire staff shortly before a meeting is held to discuss the results. If the teachers have the forms one or two days in advance of the staff meeting, they will have sufficient time to check the blanks and return them to one teacher for tabulation. A summary of the ratings can be listed on the blackboard and the blanks returned to the teachers for discussion at a staff meeting. If the staff is large, it may be desirable to form several discussion groups with teachers from every grade level participating in each group.

The check list can be divided into several areas and have several different kinds of items. The following items are illustrative of the type which might be used in that section of the check list designed to survey the inventory service.

1. Are cumulative records maintained for all students in each of the following grades? (Encircle those which apply):
   7 8 9 10 11 12
2. Is the information about students for inclusion in the cumulative record gathered by means of (check those used):
   Personal data blanks or questionnaires? ....
   Academic aptitude tests (intelligence)? ....
   Personality tests or problem check lists? ....
   Periodic health and physical examinations? ....
   Autobiographies? ....
   Reading tests? ....
   Interviews? ....
   Sociometric studies? ....
   Teacher ratings? ....
   Anecdotal records? ....
   Achievement tests? ....
   Interest tests? ....
3. In terms of the staff and student need for information about students, how complete are the cumulative records as a whole? (Check one)

Very complete ....
Somewhat complete ....
Barely adequate for minimum needs ....
Somewhat incomplete ....
Very incomplete ....

STUDENT ANALYSIS OF PRESENT SERVICES

Since the quidance program is designed to assist the student, it is only logical that he should have an opportunity to evaluate present services and to point out the need for any that are missing. Information of this kind is frequently the most effective data for establishing in the minds of all staff members the need for improved guidance services. If it is necessary to gain public support for the program, the information from the students' evaluation should prove exceedingly helpful in bringing this about.

Either the student analysis form prepared locally or a standardized problem check list can be used. It may be desirable to use both methods to obtain student opinions, attitudes, and problems. For this purpose it usually is more effective if students are not asked to identify themselves on the blank. When this procedure is followed, the student is more inclined to be frank in his answers and to contribute information one would not get otherwise.

The form prepared by the school should be so constructed as to permit a wide coverage of areas and be easy to check. Questions which can be answered by "yes" or "no" with an undecided category are often quite satisfactory. The following items are illustrative of the types of items which can be used to obtain student reaction to the breadth of the guidance services:

1. Have you found that you can talk freely about any problem with one or more of your teachers?
2. Have you received help in analyzing various college curriculums?
3. Do you need help in learning how to study?
4. Have you found that persons of the opposite sex are hard to get along with?
5. Do you feel that you have many friends among the opposite sex?

6. Do you have a problem you would like to talk over with a school person (teacher, counselor, principal, etc.)?
7. Would you like to have the school help you get a part-time job?
8. Do you know what job opportunities there are in your community?
9. Would you like to know more about how to become a leader in your group?
10. Are you concerned about going "steady?"

administration of the guidance program

PROVIDING LEADERSHIP

In the early stages of the guidance program the coordinating council usually serves in a leadership capacity. The council, as a general rule, is made up of interested teachers, administrators, and others appointed from the various special services. It has the primary responsibility for the integration and coordination of the growing program. Although the council usually is appointed by a line officer, the principal or superintendent, it is an advisory body and does not enjoy the line authority necessary for initiating its own plans. It is at this point that guidance programs reach an impasse in their development. Some means must be found in every school to give the guidance program active and understanding leadership by an individual with line authority or the program will, at best, be very slow in developing.

Line authority in the typical secondary school is vested in the principal who in turn is responsible to the superintendent of schools. These administrators are directly responsible for the implementation of the guidance program, but they are also faced with many other administrative responsibilities. Since the principal is the chief line officer of the school, it is necessary to organize the guidance staff in such a manner as to facilitate maximum benefit for the students yet permit the principal time to carry out his other administrative duties. A plan of organization which delegates line authority to another individual responsible for organizing and administering the guidance program and related activities is a desirable solution to the problem. Two suggested plans are outlined in Figure 20 and Figure 21. Assigned responsibilities have been delegated in such a manner as to

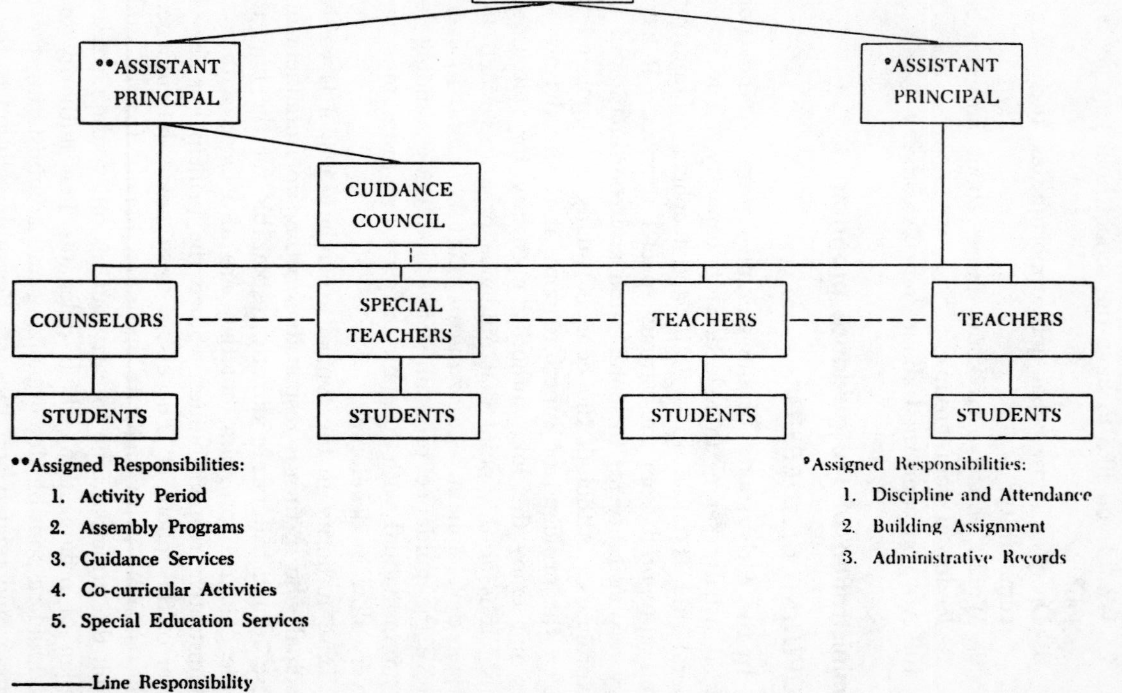
ORGANIZATIONAL RESPONSIBILITIES
Large School
PRINCIPAL
**ASSISTANT PRINCIPAL
*ASSISTANT PRINCIPAL
GUIDANCE COUNCIL
COUNSELORS
SPECIAL TEACHERS
TEACHERS
TEACHERS
STUDENTS
STUDENTS
STUDENTS
STUDENTS
**Assigned Responsibilities:
1. Activity Period
2. Assembly Programs
3. Guidance Services
4. Co-curricular Activities
5. Special Education Services
*Assigned Responsibilities:
1. Discipline and Attendance
2. Building Assignment
3. Administrative Records
Line Responsibility
Staff Responsibility

Figure 20

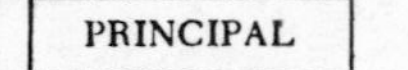

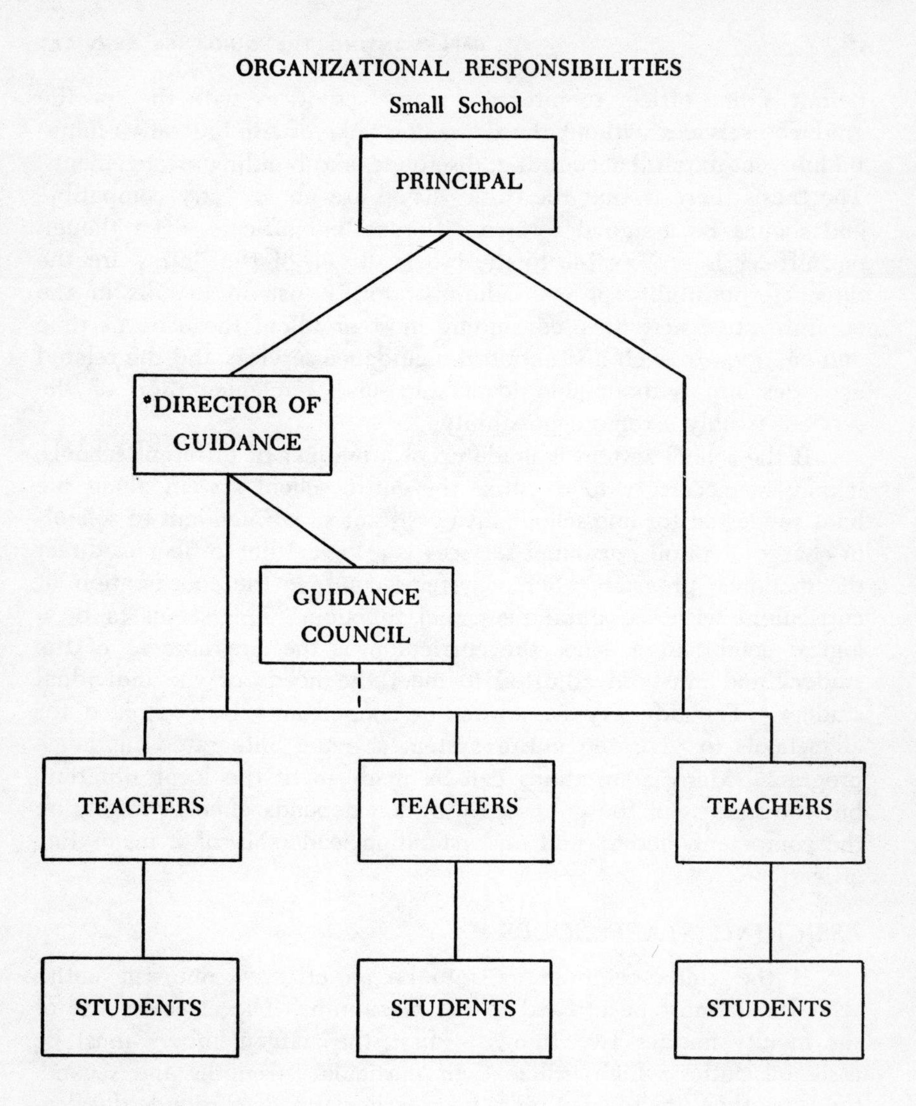

*Assigned Responsibilities:

1. Guidance Services
2. Co-curricular Activities
3. Assembly Programs

———Line Responsibility ....Staff Responsibility

Figure 21

permit a line officer to integrate many activitiees with the specific guidance services without the damaging yoke of administrative minutia inherent in pupil accounting, discipline, and building arrangements. The thesis there is that the duties listed are not directly compatible and should be assigned to two different line officers, even though one officer is responsible to the other. If all of the duties are the direct responsibility of one administrator, it usually results in the administrative activities' consuming most or all of the officer's time and energy. In such a situation the guidance services and the related activities are without line leadership and implementation of the services is only a remote possibility.

If the school system is made up of a number of different schools, it may be necessary to organize the entire school system along the lines suggested for one school. An assistant superintendent of schools in charge of pupil personnel services is a logical line officer to direct the guidance program. Some systems combine the coordination of curriculum with the pupil personnel function. This seems to be a logical combination, since the curriculum is the environment of the student and must be adjusted to meet the needs of the individual student. The advisory committee or council may be organized for all schools to give the entire system a better integrated guidance program. Many adaptations can be made to fit the local situation, but the success of the guidance program depends almost entirely on the competent, active, and understanding leadership of a major line officer.

ASSIGNING STAFF ROLES

If the guidance program is to be an effective one, the entire school staff must be utilized to the maximum. The effective use of the faculty implies two things – first, the staff members must be assigned duties which utilize their particular strengths and second, the roles they are to play must be clearly defined to reduce duplication of effort and possible friction. It often is difficult to ascertain the individual strengths of the staff unless they volunteer to function in some capacity. If the teacher has an interest in attempting some guidance project, it is usually advisable to help him define his efforts and keep them within the typical role expected of a teacher in the guidance program. The guidance functions of the classroom teacher and the counselor were discussed in Unit Five. The secondary school principal also has a unique and important role to play.

the role of the secondary school principal[2]

After the guidance program has been established, its success or failure will depend, to a large extent, upon the support it gets from the principal and his office. In junior and senior high schools that do not have a guidance specialist designated as the coordinator of these services, most of the administrative duties associated with the guidance program must be carried out by the principal. Where there is a specially trained person in charge of the guidance program, the role of the principal becomes a somewhat different one. He is then primarily responsible for:

1. Encouraging the teachers to define the purposes and the philosophy of the guidance program and creating the conditions within the school which will allow it to become an integral part of the total educational program.
2. Providing active leadership through personal support of the guidance program.
3. Defining staff roles and finding competent people to fill all guidance positions.
4. Seeking financial support for the guidance program through the superintendent's office.
5. Providing suitable physical facilities for counseling and guidance materials.
6. Counseling with individual students who seek his assistance when he has the necessary training and time.
7. Supporting a continuous evaluation of the guidance services and changes in them when they are found to be necessary.
8. Encouraging all staff members to participate in continuous in-service training projects related to guidance programs.

PROVIDING ADEQUATE SPACE

A very common question asked of guidance workers is "How much space do you need?" A quick answer suggesting a certain footage in a certain location would be a very presumptuous answer in any situation. An analysis of the need for space based on the services to be rendered is a far more realistic approach. Some of the guidance services may be provided through the typical classroom,

[2]Adapted from Raymond N. Hatch and James W. Costar. *Guidance Services in the Elementary School.* Dubuque, Iowa: Wm. C. Brown Company Publishers, 1961.

some may use space provided for some other activity, while others may require space definitely assigned to that particular service. An example of the latter type is the counseling service. The exact location of the counseling offices and the number of offices are dependent upon many factors, but a careful study of the counseling service planned for students should prove very helpful in arriving at an answer to the need for space. An example of one office arrangement is included in Figure 22.

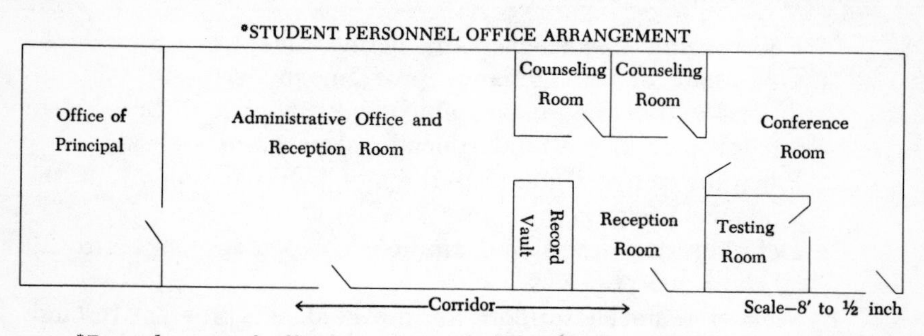

*Reproduction of office arrangement of Marysville, Michigan, High School. Reproduced through courtesy of the administrative staff.

Figure 22

UTILIZING COMMUNITY RESOURCES

The most effective guidance program uses all of the services that are available to students from outside the school to supplement those that exist within the system. This procedure is not only more effective, but it is usually more efficient as well. The scope of the services can be dramatically increased simply by using resources that are available in the local community. Educators are very quick to recognize the importance of integrating community resources with the instructional program but often fail to see that some agencies and residents in the community can be valuable extensions of the guidance program. Coordinating the guidance work of the school with similar services to students located elsewhere in the community is one of the most important and difficult administrative tasks related to the guidance program.

COMMUNITY RESOURCES AVAILABLE TO SCHOOLS

There are a wide variety of community resources available to most schools. A popular practice in larger communities during recent years has been to develop city-wide directories of social services available to adults and children. Those that are most valuable to the guidance worker fall in one of four broad categories. The categories are people, organizations, agencies, and institutions. The following are examples:

1. People
   A. Consultants (psychologists, psychiatrists, social workers, doctors, nurses, lawyers, etc.)
   B. Lecturers (travelers, representatives of certain occupations, health officers, government officials, etc.)
2. Organizations
   A. Service organizations (Rotary, Kiwanis, Lions, etc.)
   B. Professional organizations (state and local education associations, medical and dental associations, bar associations, etc.)
   C. Industrial organizations (manufacturers' associations, producers' associations, transportation associations, etc.)
   D. Business organizations (Chamber of Commerce, merchants' associations, etc.)
   E. Labor organizations (local, state, and national unions, workers' federations, etc.)
   F. Fraternal organizations (lodges, fraternities, sororities, etc.)
   G. Social organizations (clubs, societies, hobby groups, etc.)
3. Agencies
   A. Social agencies (Boy Scouts, Girl Scouts, Catholic Service Bureau, Urban League, Family Service Agency, Jewish Community League, etc.)
   B. Government agencies (child guidance clinics, state and local courts, state employment service, social welfare departments, etc.)
4. Institutions
   A. Public (universities, colleges, hospitals, technical institutes, libraries, etc.)
   B. Private (churches, colleges, vocational schools, hospitals, etc.)

Very often a school will want to develop its own community resources directory. A major advantage is that the names of individuals in private business can be included. The city directories usually list only agencies and organizations. A good practice to follow in making a school directory is to type the name of the agency, organization, or resource person, together with other pertinent data, on a five by eight inch card for easy reference. This procedure makes it possible to keep the information up to date at all times. Figure 23 shows the kind of data that is most useful and the way it might appear on the card.

COMMUNITY GUIDANCE RESOURCES

Agency or Specialist .... Data Recorded ....
Name Date

Address ....
Street Room

....
City County State

Telephone ....
Number City

Business Hours ....
Week Days Week Ends

Contact Person ....
Name Position

Services Offered ....

....

....

Fee Charges ....

Persons Eligible ....

Comments (See reverse side for additional comments regarding the agency or specialist)

Figure 23

making referrals to community agencies[3]

Contacts made by guidance workers with community agencies are often made through referrals of students for special help. A good

[3]Adapted from Raymond N. Hatch and James W. Costar. *Guidance Services in the Elementary School.* Dubuque, Iowa: Wm. C. Brown Company Publishers, 1961.

referral is a much more complicated task than simply giving the parents of a student the name and address of an agency that will assist them. Many times the child or his parents first must be helped to see that he could profit from some additional help and why it is that the school is not in the best position to offer this service. After the parents of a secondary school child have been motivated to seek special assistance for their youngster, the school should maintain a continuing relationship that will help them locate the best assistance available, obtain it for their child, and minimize the disrupting influence such activities may have on the child's school relationships.

All too often secondary school teachers are reluctant to refer a student to someone else for the help he needs. Such reluctance is not always unfounded. It may be that the referral experience itself would have a more undesirable effect on a child than the original difficulty that prompted the teacher to suggest the referral. Occasionally the teacher who makes a number of referrals is viewed as weak and inadequate by his colleagues or principal. Whatever the reason for their hesitancy, professional educators are responsible for referring pupils to appropriate people, either within or outside the school, whenever the problem requires competencies beyond their level of training and experience or is not the type of problem for which they would normally be held responsible. Referrals should be made whenever the need arises, and it is the principal's responsibility to create the kind of atmosphere which will reduce any resistance or hesitancy that staff members might have toward making them. The following are some suggestions which should help improve the referral process involving agencies outside the school system:

1. Make sure that there are no resource people in the school who can provide the assistance the student needs.
2. Do not refer a student to some agency outside the school until his parents have been fully informed and are willing to cooperate.
3. Try to reduce any anxiety which the student or his parents might have about the referral that would keep them from maintaining their contact with the agency or specialist long enough to resolve the problem.
4. Discuss the case with the referral agency before suggesting a referral to the parents. It may be that the agency is already working with the family in some other capacity.

5. Make sure the parents understand the reason for making the referral and just what services are available before they contact the agency or specialist.
6. Encourage parents to make their own appointments, thus assuring greater chances for success.
7. Secure the written consent of the parents before releasing information about the student to a community agency; this is an advisable procedure.
8. Be certain the referral is specific about names, dates, times and locations, as the student is more likely to follow through if it is.
9. Arrange to have a written or oral report from the agency on their plans for handling the case after the initial contact.
10. Maintain the kind of relationship that will make the student feel free to return to you if his contact with the referral agency is not a satisfying one.

setting realistic goals

Setting realistic goals is of paramount importance when the staff considers starting a guidance program. In many schools, it may be several years before all of the services are offered to students. In some schools it is possible to build on the present services and develop a very effective program within a relatively short time. The speed with which the program develops is directly related to such factors as the present services, the administrative leadership, the interest and qualifications of the staff, and the type of program established to implement the services. Because these variables are difficult to judge, the goals of accomplishment must be ascertained by each school. An objective each staff should consider is that of setting a goal it can reach in an effective manner.

When the organizational or implementation aspect of the guidance program is discussed, many educators are prone to think only in terms of additional costs. Any clear-thinking individual must agree that costs are important considerations, but all too frequently this is the door behind which the uninformed are inclined to hide. A large portion of the guidance program can be implemented at an additional cost of a few cents per pupil if there is a genuine desire on the part of the staff to offer such services. Most of the inventory service, much of the information service, and all of the follow-up and evaluation service can be developed at very little cost and no additional personnel. Young people in today's secondary schools deserve to come in contact with a school staff willing to carry the guidance program to the true limits of the school's resources. A school staff dedicated to the improved academic and social adjustment of young people will not rest until all of the services are available to all students. This is a desirable goal for the educational program in the secondary school. A school staff which sets a goal short of this objective must admit at the outset that effective educational experiences for all youth are of secondary importance.

summary

Guidance services exist to some degree in every secondary school. Failure of the school staff to recognize this usually is because there is no clearly defined philosophy or objectives of the guidance program. One of the first steps to be taken in the improvement of guidance services is to coordinate those that already exist. Assigning responsibility for coordinating all such activities is one of the most important guidance functions of the high school principal. In addition, he must actively seek sufficient facilities and qualified staff to insure that each student will receive the best assistance possible.

The most effective guidance program utilizes the services of teachers and administrators as well as counselors. Many secondary school teachers still feel that they are inadequately trained in the use of the various guidance techniques. A continuous in-service training program for classroom teachers is an essential aspect of any plan to initiate or improve a secondary school guidance program. An effective technique to help the staff become aware of the function of and need for guidance services is the case conference.

There are many community resources which can be used to extend and improve the guidance services of the school. These resources are widely used in the instructional program, but their value to the guidance program is too often overlooked. Consultants, social agencies, and organizations can all be used to improve guidance services. It is to be hoped that such services for pupils will increase the effectiveness of the total school program and provide each child with a better opportunity for developing his potentialities to their maximum without destroying the uniqueness of his own personality.

selected readings

An Approach to the Use of Community Agencies. Los Angeles: Los Angeles City Schools, Division of Instructional Services, Counseling and Guidance Service Branch, 1955.

Andrew, Dean D. and Willey, Roy D. *Administration and Organization of the Guidance Program.* New York: Harper and Brothers, 1958.

Community Surveys for Educational Purposes. State College, Mississippi: Industrial Education Department, Mississippi State College, 1953.

Hatch, Raymond N. and Stefflre, Buford. *Administration of Guidance Services,* Englewood Cliffs, New Jersey: Prentice-Hall, Inc., 1958.

Hulslander, Stewart C. *Utilizing Community Resources in a Program of Guidance Services.* Ann Arbor, Michigan: The Ann Arbor Publishers, 1951.

Morris, Glyn. *A Guidance Program for Rural Schools,* Chicago: Science Research Associates, Inc., 1955.

Roeber, Edward C., Smith, Glenn E., and Erickson, Clifford E. *Organization and Administration of Guidance Services.* New York: McGraw-Hill Book Company, Inc., 1955.

Stoops, Emery. *Guidance Services: Organization and Administration.* New York: McGraw-Hill Book Company, Inc., 1959.

Zeran, Franklin R. and Riccio, Anthony C. *Organizatioin and Administration of Guidance Services.* Chicago: Rand McNally and Company, 1962.

Appendix A: The Case of Paul[1]

introduction[2]

One of the requisites of an effective guidance program is the active and interested participation of the entire school staff. This cannot be accomplished without bringing staff members together for mutual discussion and study of their respective roles in such a program.

Among the various techniques which are employed for in-service programs designed to further teachers' understanding of guidance responsibilities is the case study or case conference. This technique is most effective when the "case" is one of the students from the teachers' classes. However, for purposes of introducing this method to a teaching staff or a guidance class, and for stimulating discussion, the "Case of Paul" provides an opportunity to introduce many of the aspects and considerations which must be taken into account when studying the individual. The test questions which accompany the data are designed more to promote discussion than to serve as a measure of achievement. It is suggested that the test be mimeographed and distributed to faculty members prior to a staff meeting.

---

[1]*The Case of Paul.* Guidance Staff. East Lansing, Michigan: College of Education, Michigan State University, 1956.

[2]The first edition was prepared by Jack L. Cushman and Walter F. Johnson.

The following mean scores were obtained in selected education classes at Michigan State University:

155 students in their first education course 15.6
173 students in the beginning educational psychology course 16.8
195 students in the beginning guidance course 18.9
68 students in advanced counseling laboratory courses 22.6

Paul — case study

IDENTIFYING DATA

Paul is 18 years of age and an 11th grade student. He has come to see you, a teacher-counselor, because he says that he is dissatisfied with his marks. He states that perhaps you can help him by suggesting some study techniques. A full-time, trained counselor is available in the school.

HOME AND FAMILY BACKGROUND

Paul and his family moved into Silver City two years ago. His father is a traveling salesman for a manufacturing concern. Neither of his parents completed high school. He has an older brother (age 21) who is attending the state university and majoring in engineering. Paul's parents were separated for a short time since moving into Silver City. There is neighborhood gossip that another separation is imminent. They are living together at the present time. Paul and his mother attend events in the community together. The father rarely accompanies them. According to the mother, the older brother is on the college honor roll and will be graduating from college in June.

PREVIOUS SCHOOL EXPERIENCE AND PRESENT SCHOOL RECORD

Paul attended elementary and junior high school in a small town. He entered his present school in the 10th grade. The students in the school he is now attending have high average scholastic ability. His class had an average I.Q. of 112 in a group intelligence test administered in the 10th grade.

Records from the previous schools reveal marks of about a "B" average: English – B; Mathematics – B; Social Studies – B; Industrial Arts – A.

Records also indicate that Paul was a "model" student while in the former school. While in Silver City High School he has been somewhat of a disciplinary problem. He has been reprimanded for smoking on the school grounds and taking part in unauthorized hazing of freshmen students. His marks in the Silver City High School have been as follows:

Grade 10	Grade 11
English – C	English – C
Geometry – C	U. S. History – B
Biology – C	Geometry – C
World History – C	Science – C

Paul has been a member of the History and Travel clubs and is now in the Speech club. He has served on numerous school committees. His teachers report that he has not always fulfilled his duties on these committees. Teachers also report that Paul has a tendency to stutter when reciting before the class.

There are a number of anecdotal records in his personnel folder. They contain such statements as: "Paul is extremely lazy in preparing his lessons," "Paul is always starting fights," "Paul is always seeking attention," "Paul recently had a fight with Jim, a classmate of his." During the course of a conversation with his teacher-counselor, Paul stated that he and some other boys skipped school a short time ago and wrote their own excuses.

TEST DATA	*I.Q.*
Kuhlmann-Anderson Intelligence Test – 5th grade	101
Otis Self-Administering Test of Mental Ability, Higher Form – 9th grade	115
Iowa Tests of Educational Development – 10th grade (Silver City High School Norms)	Percentile
Understanding of Basic Social Concepts	72
Background in Natural Science	41
Correctness in Writing	28
Ability to do Quantitative Thinking	56
Ability to Interpret Reading Materials in the Social Studies	58
Ability to Interpret Reading Materials in the Natural Sciences	53
Ability to Interpret Literary Materials	40

General Vocabulary 46
Use of Sources of Information 18

Kuder Preference Record – 11th grade – percentile scores (national norms)

Mechanical	88	Social Service	31
Persuasive	93	Scientific	89
Musical	50	Literary	65
Computational	16	Clerical	10
Artistic	44		

Bell Adjustment Inventory – 11th grade
Home Adjustment – average
Health Adjustment – good
Social Adjustment – aggressive
Emotional Adjustment – unsatisfactory

HEALTH AND SOCIAL

Paul is 5′11″ and weighs 160 pounds. He has been absent from school for what his mother describes as sinus headaches. Glasses were worn while in the earlier grades, but not since attending Silver City High School. Paul's mother also reports that lately Paul has been crying himself to sleep while sucking his thumb.

Since shortly after the beginning of this semester, Paul has been going "steady" with a girl of non-Protestant faith. Paul's mother has not approved since Paul is Protestant.

Paul has stated that he used to attend church and take an active part in church activities. Lately, Paul's church attendance has been infrequent.

GOALS

Paul has indicated that he desires to study mechanical engineering. In the 9th grade Paul had prepared a career book in which he studied baseball as a career. Also, in the 10th grade a lawyer spoke to his class and Paul changed his goal from baseball to law. Since his brother has been in college Paul has changed his choice to engineering.

discussion questions

The following questions require application of information contained in the case study of Paul. Read all questions carefully. Refer

to the case study if necessary. There is only *one* best answer for each question. Answer all questions.

Make no marks on this paper. Place all answers on the answer sheet.

1. As a teacher-counselor, your first job when beginning to counsel with Paul would be to:
   A. administer tests to determine the area of difficulty.
   B. establish a good working relationship.
   C. determine if there is a need for a conference.
   D. have Paul write out his problem for clarification.
   E. call Paul's parents so they will be aware of proceedings.
2. As a teacher-counselor, to whom Paul has come for help, one of your first steps would be to:
   A. send Paul to the school counselor as he has had more training in counseling with students.
   B. give Paul an assignment so that you can study his work habits.
   C. conduct your study from the present as every student deserves a fresh start.
   D. administer a standardized achievement test to be sure his grades are justified.
   E. examine his past records for indications of difficulty and strength.
3. When Paul first came to your office you should have:
   A. assumed that achieving better grades is the main problem.
   B. taken steps to obtain help in remedial reading since low reading ability is a common cause of poor grades.
   C. been alert for any evidence of problems other than grades.
   D. called the parents for a conference or made a home visit.
   E. asked the school counselor to come in for a joint conference.
4. In view of the apparent family conflict, it would probably be best for you to:
   A. talk to the parents and try to keep Paul from being the victim of a broken home.
   B. try to arrange for Paul to live with his father as he needs the association of another man.

C. persuade the mother to move from the city with Paul so as to leave unpleasant associations behind.
D. take no direct action in attempting a reconciliation of the parents.
E. talk to the father and try to get him to change his ways.

5. When Paul told you that he skipped school and signed his own excuse you should have:
A. notified the principal or superintendent so that they can take administrative action.
B. called the other boys to be certain they were guilty.
C. kept the confidence.
D. notified the parents.
E. told Paul that he must admit this to all concerned.

6. You have evidence on Paul's intelligence to indicate that:
A. there is probably no serious discrepancy between his subject matter achievement and intelligence level.
B. Paul is above the average intelligence in his class.
C. Paul's intelligence is improving.
D. Paul should be doing better work in school.
E. Paul has been receiving unjustified grades.

7. The difference in the two I.Q. scores:
A. probably is an indication that Paul's intelligence is increasing.
B. is of no significance.
C. is evidence that when administering a second intelligence test it should be by the same author as the first.
D. indicates that the Otis was better administered than the Kuhlmann-Anderson.
E. may be an indication that Paul's reading ability has improved.

8. Considering the information available on Paul's intelligence it would be advisable to:
A. administer another intelligence test to define more clearly his intelligence.
B. administer another intelligence test and then average all three scores.
C. ignore the information as the discrepancy in scores makes the tests valueless.
D. ignore the first test and consider only the more recent one.

E. administer another intelligence test to see if his reading ability is still improving.

9. The information on the achievement tests indicates that:
   A. Paul should be set back at least one grade so that he can catch up with the other students.
   B. Paul needs remedial work in some areas.
   C. Paul's school grades have been too high.
   D. either the intelligence test scores or the achievement test scores are incorrect.
   E. Paul is weak in nearly all areas.
10. A study of the Kuder scores indicates that:
   A. 10 per cent of a group are more interested in clerical duties than Paul.
   B. Paul answered 65 per cent of the questions concerning literary interests.
   C. Paul is more interested in mechanical duties than 12 per cent of his fellow students.
   D. Paul is in the second quartile in artistic interests.
   E. Paul has more aptitude for social service work than clerical work.
11. The results of the Kuder Preference Record also indicate that:
   A. Paul has some aptitude for mechanical work.
   B. Paul wouldn't be very interested in many of the activities performed by an office clerk.
   C. Paul is twice as interested in mechanical work as he is in artistic work.
   D. Paul would do well in debate.
   E. Paul would probably make a good salesman.
12. Considering the information available in the Bell Adjustment Inventory, you should:
   A. inform the parents of the results so that they will realize there is a serious problem.
   B. obtain the scores for the areas tested and average his total adjustment.
   C. examine the individual items so as to identify further the problem areas.
   D. establish the validity of Paul's responses.
   E. go over the scores with Paul.

13. The available evidence indicates that Paul at present is probably:
    A. an underachiever.
    B. an overachiever.
    C. achieving up to his level of ability.
    D. working only in areas of his interests.
    E. achieving only in the easier subjects.
14. In using the test data available, it would be best to:
    A. have the parents look over the scores so that any interpretation will be their responsibility.
    B. explain to Paul that he is above average intelligence for his group.
    C. have the parents see Paul's high scores first.
    D. present your interpretation of the data to Paul and his parents.
    E. have the parents look over Paul's responses on the Bell Adjustment Inventory so that they can see where they have failed as parents.
15. The total information indicates that:
    A. Paul is in need of special help in all areas of his school work.
    B. special remedial work is unnecessary.
    C. Paul is a poor reader for his group.
    D. Paul's grades are too low for his ability.
    E. Paul needs special help with work in certain areas.
16. As a teacher dealing with Paul's stuttering in the classroom it would be best for you to:
    A. have Paul recite only when he desired.
    B. insist that Paul recite often so that he will get over his nervousness.
    C. explain to Paul that there is no reason for him to stutter as he should not be nervous.
    D. treat his stuttering by having him repeat sentences.
    E. have Paul's mother treat his difficulty in the more natural home surroundings.
17. There is evidence that Paul:
    A. is abnormally unstable in the selection of a vocation.
    B. would fit into many different occupations.
    C. is following a normal pattern of job selection for adolescents.

D. should listen to speakers representing many occupations.
E. needs someone else to diagnose his capabilities and decide for him his best choice of occupations.

18. A reliability coefficient of .92 is reported for the Otis Self-Administering test of Mental Ability; this means that:
A. 92 per cent of the items test mental ability.
B. 92 per cent of those taking the test receive valid scores.
C. that we can predict the success in intellectual pursuits of 92 per cent of the people who take the test.
D. there is evidence that the test measures consistently.
E. the test is a good measure of intelligence.

19. Considering the "thumb sucking and crying himself to sleep," you have evidence that:
A. Paul is trying to get attention from his father.
B. Paul's intelligence is lower than the intelligence tests indicate.
C. Paul's early childhood was probably his unhappiest period.
D. Paul is insecure.
E. Paul is adjusting through the mechanism of pseudo-feeblemindedness.

20. Paul's "model" behavior in the former school can most likely be attributed to:
A. higher status among the students at that school.
B. his better grades and the resulting less frustration.
C. a curriculum that met his needs better.
D. different standards of behavior in the two schools.
E. less emotional stress at that period.

21. Probably the least serious bit of evidence we have is:
A. his aggressive behavior in class.
B. the "thumb sucking and crying himself to sleep."
C. the lower grades he has received in Silver City High School.
D. his stuttering in class.
E. his skipping school.

22. Of the following, the most serious bit of evidence is probably:
A. the hazing of the freshmen.
B. the lower grades in Silver City High School .
C. his aggressive behavior in class.

D. absence from school because of repeated headaches.
E. his "thumbsucking and crying himself to sleep."

23. In the instance when Paul and Jim were fighting, it would have been best to:
A. stop the fight and talk to them later.
B. send them down to the gymnasium to put on the gloves.
C. send them to the principal who should handle serious discipline problems.
D. insist that Paul apologize for starting the fight.
E. settle the issue immediately.

24. An acceptable procedure in overcoming Paul's refusal to recite in class would be to:
A. impress upon Paul's parents the importance of reciting in class.
B. ask some of Paul's friends to show approval whenever Paul does recite.
C. read off the names of those who have not recited.
D. build his confidence by recognition of work he has done.
E. make an agreement with Paul to ask him only easy questions.

25. Considering the type of anecdotal records that are available, you as a teacher-counselor, should:
A. consider the anecdotal records valuable since the other teachers have determined the basis for some of Paul's main problems.
B. present Paul with these statements so as to hear his side of the story.
C. question the value of the anecdotal records as evidence of his present status.
D. consider them as your objective evidence.
E. present the parents with the records.

26. If Paul's parents were consulted, it would be most desirable to say:
A. "We find that students' problems in school frequently stem from the home."
B. "I can help Paul with your cooperation."
C. "I would like to settle this since Paul is holding back the rest of the class."
D. "I am interested in helping Paul."
E. "Our tests indicate that Paul needs help."

27. Which of the following is the safest prognosis of Paul's academic success in college?
    A. It is quite likely that Paul would not succeed.
    B. Success would depend to a considerable degree upon emotional adjustment.
    C. Going to college would motivate him to do better work.
    D. He would probably be successful, but not in engineering.
    E. Success would depend upon the extent of his social and extra-curricular activities.
28. As a teacher-counselor, which of the following would be best for you to consider as a part of a program to help Paul?
    A. Help Paul to improve his grades to his previous level of accomplishment.
    B. Attempt to reconcile the parental differences.
    C. Reduce the apparent emotional tension.
    D. Try to get Paul's brother to take an active interest in him.
    E. Help Paul to recognize and accept the incompatability of his parents.

MOST FREQUENT RESPONSES

1. B	7. E	13. C	19. D	25. C
2. E	8. A	14. D	20. E	26. D
3. C	9. B	15. E	21. C	27. B
4. D	10. D	16. A	22. E	28. C
5. C	11. B	17. C	23. A	
6. A	12. C	18. D	24. D	

Subject Index

A

B

C

D

E

J

L

M

N

O

S

T

U

V

W